T0196900

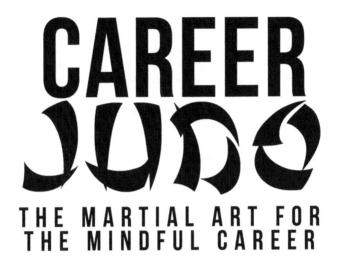

CAREER JUDO

THE MARTIAL ART FOR THE MINDFUL CAREER

JOHN E. LONG, ED.S.
WITH ERIN NEWMAN

BALBOA.
PRESS
A DIVISION OF HAY HOUSE

Balboa Press books may be ordered through booksellers or by contacting:

Balboa Press
A Division of Hay House
1663 Liberty Drive
Bloomington, IN 47403
www.balboapress.com
1 (877) 407-4847

Print information available on the last page.

ISBN: 978-1-5043-8476-6 (sc)
ISBN: 978-1-5043-8478-0 (hc)
ISBN: 978-1-5043-8477-3 (e)

Library of Congress Control Number: 2017911747

Balboa Press rev. date: 09/01/2017

CONTENTS

INFLUENCES AND
ACKNOWLEDGEMENTS

T he following individuals have made some astounding contributions to our World. Their collective works will forever inspire and guide my journey on this beautiful *Big Blue Marble* (yes, I adore *PBS*).

Richard Bolles, S.T.M. (1927 to 2017) was an ordained Episcopal minister, writer and presenter. He will forever be cherished as the pioneering author of the best-seller *What Color is Your Parachute?*

Markus Buckingham, M.A. encourages us to ignite our potential through several ground breaking books, including *Now, Discover Your Strengths* and *Go Put Your Strengths to Work.*

Leo Buscaglia, Ph.D. (1924 - 1998) was the author of *Born for Love*, one of his many popular books. His words of wisdom, "life is our greatest possession and love its greatest affirmation", are timeless.

Albert Ellis, Ph.D. (1913 to 2007) was a clinical psychologist credited with the development of Rational Emotive Behavioral Therapy. REBT is a therapeutic approach used to challenge self-sabotaging beliefs and replace them with positive, affirming thoughts to support emotional well-being and goal attainment.

Laura Berman Fortgang, MCC authored *Now What? 90 Days to a New Life Direction* (one of her many powerful books), which will forever elevate my work.

Viktor Frankl, M.D., Ph.D. (1905 - 1997) was a Holocaust survivor and the author of several ground-breaking publications, including *Man's Search for Meaning.*

Judith Grutter, M.S. (1942 - 2014) was an accomplished and gifted counselor and trainer. Her work with the *MBTI®* and *Strong Interest Inventory®* has touched, and will continue to benefit, countless lives.

John Holland, Ph.D. (1919 - 2008) gave us the Holland Occupational Themes model of career development. The Holland Codes now serve as a cornerstone of career assessment and exploration.

Carl G. Jung, M.D. (1875 - 1961) is the founder of analytical psychology and author of *Psychological Types,* one of his many innovative works.

Richard Knowdell, M.S. created incredible card sort assessments, which are both fun and enlightening.

Sonja Lyubomirsky, Ph.D. shared her work, *The How of Happiness*, with the world. This book has become my mantra and my compass.

Abraham Maslow, Ph.D. (1908 - 1970) is the creator of *Maslow's Hierarchy of Needs*, a five tiered model of human needs, culminating in self-actualization.

Frank Parsons (1854 - 1908) worked as a civil engineer, writer, teacher, and professor, and was widely regarded for his overarching role as a social reformer. Parsons' revolutionary book, *Choosing a Vocation*, solidified his place in history as the father of the vocational guidance movement.

Christopher Peterson, Ph.D. (1950 - 2012) was a key figure in the field of positive psychology. He authored *A Primer in Positive Psychology* and spearheaded the *VIA Survey of Character Strengths*.

Mark Savickas, Ph.D. developed *Career Construction Theory*, which captivates me and informs my work. As Dr. Savickas often says, "we must actively master what we passively suffer".

Martin Seligman, Ph.D., the father of Positive Psychology, is a personal idol. He has reached my head, heart and soul, through his *PERMA* model and publications, including *Authentic Happiness* and *Flourish*.

"Face your fear, empty yourself, trust your own voice, let go of control, have faith in outcomes, connect with a larger purpose, derive meaning from the struggle."

- Jigaro Kano, the founder of Judo

SPECIAL THANKS

A few years ago, I had the pleasure of working with a gifted life coach who challenged me by asking me a deep question: What did I think my legacy might be? At first, I was completely stumped by how to answer. I don't have children to carry my name and memory forward, and that made my response even more elusive. When I look back, I recognize that I am the product of a pretty amazing childhood. I was nurtured by teachers, neighbors, parents, and four incredibly loving grandparents. Now on the other side of mid-life, perhaps I can say that I have acquired a few trinkets of wisdom that I hold in an imaginary red velvet, satin-lined pouch, along with fond memories, and bits of patience and humility.

As I reflect upon my roles and experiences in life, I hope to be remembered by others as having created some positive ripples:

> …while sharing mat time with fellow lovers of the art, science, and gift of Judo
>
> …while helping several medical groups deliver high quality patient care
>
> …while absorbing humble wisdom from Barbara, Harry and Bill, my three cherished mentors

…while encouraging my students to inquire and share their perspectives and their voice

…while supporting my clients in their journey of discovery and growth

…while brainstorming, smiling, and listening in conversations with fellow coaches, counselors, advisors, and instructors

…while sharing love, laughter, and loyalty with my small tribe of treasured friends

…while offering encouragement to my nieces, nephews, grand-nieces, and grand-nephews

…while focusing on returning the love and trust so willingly shared by my big sister, big brother, and their families

…while feeling the warmth of unconditional love from my mom and dad—two people who have shared everything and only ask that I repay them with my happiness

…while savoring a meal, a walk, an embrace, or a moment with Ryan, the person who accepts me at my worst, elevates me, and holds my heart.

I offer my sincere thanks to all the people who have allowed me to be a part of their lives and their organizations as I took in the experience and grew from the investment of time. And I am especially grateful to my writing coach, Erin Newman, and my editor, Diane Eaton, whose gentle, persistent, guidance allowed me to complete this project.

With positivity, mindfulness, and gratitude! —John

INTRODUCTION

THE SEARCH FOR A TRUE FIT, MEANINGFUL CAREER

"Man does not simply exist but always decides what his existence
will be, what he will become the next moment. By the same token,
every human being has the freedom to change at any instant."
– Viktor E. Frankl

This book is about helping you find a true fit in your life's work.

As an adolescent, I didn't find happiness or success with traditional American sports like baseball, football, and basketball. For a time, my dad was the coach of the local little league team and, due to his well-meaning insistence, I reluctantly agreed to play on the team for a season. Not surprisingly, I failed miserably. I wanted to be good at sports, like my older brother, and connect on a deeper level with my athletic dad, but I quickly realized that my DNA just wasn't programmed that way.

Then I happened upon a book about judo at a local school book fair. The thin, simple book literally changed my life. I can't explain why I was so captivated by it, but I was. Soon enough, the binding got worn down from all the flipping back and forth through the pages that I subjected it to. Learning about the special uniform (*gi*), the colored belts (*obi*), the mystery of the Japanese culture, and the ancient traditions of a martial art created a desire to do something more than just read about judo. I found a judo class and convinced my dad to let me join. I was soon enrolled in a beginner's class in an established judo club at the local YMCA in central New York.

For me, there was a compelling allure to the practice of judo: from the training, conditioning, and respectful bows, to the instructor (*sensei*) and peers, to the traditions embodied in each technique. The classes and tournaments I attended in my teens led to a series of colored belts that celebrated my increasing skills and knowledge. As an adult, advanced training took me through three levels of brown belt, until I was finally awarded the coveted black belt. Fast-forward many years later to find me leading my own judo class.

My commitment of time and effort to this amazing practice (along with the many sprains and bruises I experienced) propelled me into adulthood; it gave me a solid foundation of self-esteem, confidence, and achievement. While I was not drawn to serious judo competition, I cherished the experience of the tournaments I entered. By finding my fit in judo, I knew I was more resourceful and resilient for whatever lay ahead.

And changes were in store for me.

I admit it: I'm a "career transition" survivor. I successfully navigated the challenges of moving from one career to another. I enjoyed successful roles in healthcare administration and I've managed several medical group practices. I'm now cultivating a career as a college and university instructor, and have over a decade of experience as a nationally certified career coach. From those experiences, I've written *Career Judo* to provide you with the fruits of what I learned along the way.

As a professional coach, my focus is on helping people live a more authentic life. I'm driven by a desire to empower others to work with the truth within them, and the resources and energy that surround them. I'm passionate about guiding jobseekers to use a combination of exploration and mindfulness to transform their work life into a career that is meaningful and continually evolving. With *Career Judo*, I hope to do this for you.

For over a decade, I have had the privilege of working with many wonderful students and clients seeking greater insight into a unique and fulfilling professional path. I genuinely believe that my experience with such a diversity of people, scenarios, and goals informs and drives my brand of career coaching. And, if you are like many of my clients, then you have a burning desire to find greater meaning in your own work: a better "fit" as you grow in your career and your life.

Career Judo combines a lifetime of insights with over a decade of practical strategies and resources that have been applied successfully by my students and clients. Like the colored belts you are awarded as you advance in judo training, this book offers step-wise levels of trusted techniques and a progression of knowledge, skills, and resources to help you achieve a meaningful change in your career. Each "belt" in *Career Judo* provides viable techniques that you can immediately engage to craft your career map and achieve results. Most importantly, just as you would learn how to balance your own unique strengths against those of your opponents in the *dojo, Career Judo* helps you discover what makes you unique in the job market and learn how to best express that to potential employers.

STREAMLINING THE CAREER SEARCH

If you're like many people, you're struggling with whether the career you're in is right for you. But when you review the literature on the subject, it all seems to come up short: either it's too esoteric, too specific, or more distressingly, unable to address your unique concerns. All too often spiritual books seem to be directed towards a Buddhist monk, or at least someone who doesn't face the daily stresses of work, home, children, and mortgages. On the other hand, career books often ask you to look deeply within for answers (which, of itself, is wonderful) without providing viable and concrete tools you need to actively manage a career search.

Perhaps the career advice you've received up until this point has simply missed the mark.

Career Judo bridges the gap by offering you practical advice if you are seeking a more mindful career journey—whether you are just starting out in the working world, in a mid-career change, or even aiming to retire and do something entirely different. *Career Judo* is meant to be a life-enhancing system that you bring with you wherever you go—exploring, leveraging, and consistently building upon. Each chapter gives real-world guidance that you can put into practice immediately, while helping you be mindful of the process of positive change. After all, if you don't know what sort of career you are seeking, then simply refreshing a resume, searching internet job boards and updating your LinkedIn profile with more general content will not likely yield the results you're seeking.

Moreover, you won't be able to write an effective resume until you have a clear sense of the role you want to pursue. A one-size-fits-all, generic resume will quickly be overlooked by employers; a targeted, accomplishment-based resume—one driven by strengths, credentials, and achievements—will showcase your unique value in a role and to an organization. With *Career Judo*, you'll learn how to refocus and leverage your current credentials (education, training, and experience) while blending in elements of your strengths, values, interests, and personality—known as the "Four Cornerstones."

The word "judo" is Japanese for "the gentle way." Like judo, the guidance in *Career Judo* can be like a match or exercise in which you acknowledge the force of your opponent— i.e. your problems—and use that force as a complement to your strengths. Instead of aggressively attacking an unwanted adversary, for example, you learn how to thoughtfully counter its force with deflection, redirection, and fluid motion.

When applied to a career search, this approach means you don't have to look at it as a high-pressure scenario and feel compelled to make a huge decision to follow one career path that will last you a lifetime. Instead, you can see it as an opportunity for growth and exploration, much as a move by an opponent in judo can be seen as a chance to apply a new technique or develop a new strength.

Judo teaches us how to transform the energy of anything that stands in "opposition" to us. In *Career Judo*, you'll utilize many of the same skills as those in the dojo, transforming what "opposes" you—whether it be the job market, a degree, a training program, a new career, a boss, or your doubts and insecurities—into something greater. You'll ultimately build a stronger, more forward-looking career.

For example, in judo we learn that it's not pure strength that can bring about an opponent's fall; it is the result of upsetting our opponent's force and balance through skill and foresight. We also learn how to fall in a safe and graceful way, and we can reengage easily, even when we don't feel at our strongest. In the same way, you'll learn how to use your unique skills in the "dojo of life" that will allow you to keep your balance, despite any opposition.

Career Judo will guide you through:

- Exercises and self-assessments pertaining to your strengths, values, interests, and personality
- Networking, career exploration, career mapping, and work-life synergy
- Exercises to research selected career paths
- Developing targeted career materials that make an impact, including resume, letters, reference sheet, and LinkedIn profiles
- Proactive job search strategies: discovering the hidden job market
- Development of the unique brand called "You"
- Successful interview techniques and self-promotional strategies
- Finding flow in your career progression
- Mindfulness techniques for successful life-long career evolution

YOU'RE IN CHARGE OF YOUR DESTINY

Through the methods you'll find in this book, you'll discover that you don't need to let passivity, complacency, and apathy derail your power to make strong career decisions. You won't simply allow or accept whatever life throws at you—in your career, your education, or your perceived notions of what you "should" be doing—to dictate the career that you want to have. You'll actively seek out opportunities for learning and growth and realize that you can take pro-active steps in your career and your life. You'll know that you have the power and ability to build a meaningful, satisfying, and multi-dimensional career. Whether that means re-crafting your current role, seeking out an environment that fits you better, or starting in an entirely new field—there is a path for you to get you to higher fulfillment. You'll learn that your power lies in the fact that you always have options to explore.

HOW TO READ THIS BOOK

You can read this book in the order presented—or not. You can certainly skip around to address your current situation. However, there is a certain progression designed into the book and you will probably get more out of it by reading and absorbing the material in that logical sequence. Each chapter heading is associated with a belt color from judo, and each chapter is meant to be seen as a stepping-stone, the completion of which marks a level of achievement on your journey. As you do your work and progress through each belt, you will understand more and more about yourself.

I have put many resources on my website **www.careerjudo.com** that can be helpful for you on your journey to find your best career fit. In this book, when you see this icon [◑] you'll find resources related to the topic online for you.

By mastering the guidance and concepts in *Career Judo*, you can use the energy and stimulus from your seeming "opponents" in life and put them in your corner; you can transform your path to a fulfilling career and acquire new knowledge about yourself. Commit to doing the necessary work, and you'll advance from white belt to black belt and progress from good to better to best career fit!

CHAPTER 1: WHITE BELT

GAINING INSIGHT AND SELF-KNOWLEDGE

"When I discover who I am, I'll be free."
— Ralph Ellison

Many people are convinced that because of a bad boss, evil coworkers, or even just a bad fit for their personality, they have to leave their current job. But it may be just that they need to re-align their focus and concentrate on those aspects of their job that they enjoy and that plays to their strengths.

That process of career course-correction is known as *job crafting*. It's when, instead of *changing* your role, you *realign* it by proactively seeking out opportunities to take on new tasks and to cultivate new interactions in your work. It's a time when you focus on the things you do well and the tasks you might enjoy. Job crafting may seem like a simple concept, but it can be very powerful because it allows you to increase the control you have over your career. As a result, you are demonstrating a desire to learn, grow, and evolve in your career, while staying with the same employer, for the present.

Try it out. Start by looking at the tasks that you currently do in your job and see if there are some that you really do enjoy. Perhaps you can trade tasks or responsibilities with a colleague, team member, or subordinate to see if you both might have more satisfaction in the trade. Also consider working on teams with others. Where can you lend your unique skills to the rest of the organization? If you start to think creatively with your tasks and roles, you may find that you are able to create the role that you've always wanted, without too much trouble, after all.

HOPPING AND HOPING

But maybe you've tried all that, or you instinctively feel like it's not the direction for you. What next? Maybe you really do need to find a new role for yourself or even a new career. If so, then take a moment and reflect on how much time you usually spend on making other major life decisions. For example, you would probably spend many hours researching which new car you want to purchase; you'd spend a good bit of time planning a European vacation; you'd take an extensive amount of time planning a major event like a wedding or a reunion. But, if you're like many others, you probably don't expect to spend the same amount of time researching a new career role. Instead, you "hop and hope": you hope that your next job hop will make you happier in your career.

Your career decisions are just as important, if not more important, than any of your other life decisions. After all, you spend the majority of your waking hours doing what you do for a living, and if you're unhappy with your job, then that unhappiness will find its way into all other aspects of your life. Just think of the last time you had a bad day at work or school. Were you able to check that negativity at the door when you came home?

Finding a career fit that is both meaningful and rewarding to you is important. Just as in judo, where muscular strength alone is not enough to succeed, you can't simply force yourself to try harder or be stronger in a job or career that is no longer rewarding or purposeful. But when you gain insight into your skills and strengths, values, interests, and personality, then you can leave the "hop and hope" approach behind you. You can learn to leverage your unique strengths to overcome perceived circumstances and forces that you believe to be working against you. And you can do this right now, regardless of where you find yourself in life.

Many people come to me for career coaching after they've already launched themselves into a career sector. They're usually seeking guidance either after they got frustrated from jobs they took following college, at a mid-life transition, or after they've been working in an industry for many years. But it's all good. It's never too late to gain insight into yourself and to discover new career paths or roles that may be a better fit for you. Whether you remain in the same industry or even the same company, learning more about what it is that you enjoy doing, and do well, can make a profound difference in all aspects of your life. Just imagine going to work every day and feeling satisfied with your job choice, having that quiet sense of knowing that what you are doing is personally meaningful and is allowing you to live a more authentic life.

So let's get started. In order to find that career fit, you'll have to invest time in what career counselors and coaches describe as the "Four Cornerstones of Career Self-Knowledge". The first "Cornerstone" is about your unique skills and strengths.

GETTING TO KNOW YOUR SKILLS AND VALUES

I can still remember the experience of walking into my first judo club even though it was 40 years ago. The floor of the room was covered in light grey *tatami* mats interwoven between several cement pillars. Each person was dressed in a *gi*, a white uniform, and was wearing the traditional *obi*, a colored belt. From the edge of the concrete room, I quietly watched the class progress, awestruck.

It was nothing like I had ever seen before.

The students bowed to each other very respectfully and then an older man wearing a black belt led the group through a variety of exercises and routines and offered demonstrations of techniques. He was the *sensei*, our judo instructor. I watched in amazement as the *judoka* (students) practiced a series of throws (*tachi waza*), which transitioned into free practice (*randori*) and grappling on the mats (*newaza*).

I was hooked; it was all I could do to stop myself from running out from the side of the room and jumping onto the mats.

Just as a judoka learns a lot by doing throws and mat work and practicing with their training partners, you can learn a lot from your career interactions, too. Whether you're responding to colleagues, peers, clients, or your boss, you can learn a lot about how to best apply your unique skills to the work at hand.

Most people tend to take a very narrow view of the skills they use on the job or in school. Then they stumble by asking the wrong questions, like, "Do I have the skill set that matches this job description? Do I have what's necessary for this assignment?" But if you try to determine your unique skill set first, and *then* look for a role that provides a solid match, you'll have much more success.

So let's start you off at the beginning by looking at your skills holistically: as a complete package. I'll take you through a series of exercises to help you see what you bring to the table—your skills, gifts, talents, and passions—in your hobbies, your volunteer activities, your place of worship or spiritual practice, your exercise or fitness routines, your family life, your community engagement, and circle of friends. What are those things that people have always told you that you've done well, both in the past and currently? You'll start to think about the total set of skills and strengths that you offer and often demonstrate.

Let's look at the different kinds of skills you have:

Transferable Skills

Transferable skills are the ones that you always have in your metaphorical backpack. They are not necessarily innate, because they, too, can be learned. However, they are the skills that you use confidently, you know that you are good at them, and others have told you that you have these skill-sets. Transferable skills are the ones that you can take with you as you move from job to job and task to task, and are not dependent upon a specific role or title. Examples would be an affinity for solving math problems, using tools to build things, being organized, and speaking to people in a friendly, confident manner.

Motivated Skills

Now, from your list of transferrable skills, select the ones that you would elevate to a higher order list of *Motivated* skills. These are the skills that you do well and also enjoy doing, hence, you are *motivated* to do them. Ultimately, you would like to see more motivated skills show up in your next job description. They are the items you are going to want to focus on.

Exercise 1: Lists of Transferrable and Motivated Skills ◑

A solid approach to determining your skills is to brainstorm a list of all of your perceived skills in all areas of your life.

Use the suggested resources at www.careerjudo.com to help you make a list of your transferrable skills. Again, they're the ones that seem to come naturally to you, whether or not it took training to learn them. Remember to look at yourself holistically: consider all your life roles. They might include being a daughter, son, wife, husband, mom, business analyst, project manner, runner, amateur musician, and a volunteer member of a community non-profit, for example. Your initial list may contain 30 or 40 entries from a variety of categories, such as analytical skills, technical skills, and communication skills. Then, from this first list, choose the skills you would consider your motivated skills, and create this critical second list. Keep this handy as you move forward with your career exploration.

***

Once you have a list of your motivated skills, keep it nearby as a reference for the rest of your job search. Use it to remind you of many motivated skills that you want your next job to include. You can tape the list next to your workstation as a daily reminder to channel your energies into uncovering the roles and environments where you may be most satisfied with the work you'll be doing.

This doesn't mean that you will need to abandon your transferable skills; they will remain in your "backpack" while you give greater attention to the items on your motivated skills list. Your motivated skills will provide the direction and guidance in your search for a career role that fits you better.

I can give you an example of this from my own life experience. In my previous career in healthcare administration, I was responsible for completing regular bookkeeping, banking, and accounting tasks. My two semesters of college accounting, my continuing education credits, and on the job training prepared me for the financial management responsibilities that ultimately represented about 60% of my job. I was very good at these tasks and could balance large budgets to the penny. Yet, over time I started to truly despise this part of my job. When I took the time to take notice of the work tasks that I truly enjoyed, I became aware of my motivated skills that had to do with training and development, mentoring, coaching, and teaching.

VALUES

In addition to other martial arts and sports, judo is known to instill strong values in youngsters, novices, and anyone else who spends time learning and practicing it. Self-discipline, humility, commitment, and determination are some of the more widely known values; even a black belt must return their focus to these precepts. Getting up after you've been knocked to the ground will instill humility in anyone!

Whether you're trained in martial arts or not, you have internalized certain core values, ideas, and beliefs about what you know to be a more authentic way of living life. When you start to think about a new job or career, you need to consider if your values are in alignment with a potential company and role. For instance, if you feel strongly about environmental sustainability, then you may not wish to work for a Styrofoam manufacturer. While that may seem obvious, many can be blinded by the trinity of "Pay, Benefits, and Title," and hesitate to look deeply into a company's culture and practices.

Many people make the mistake of approaching a career by asking, "How can I morph myself into this role and make it work?" But this is where you can easily end up hopping and hoping again, only to unwittingly land in a position that goes against what you believe to be important in life. You might even have thought that if you got everything you wanted in terms of "Pay, Benefits, and Title," that the rest would take care of itself.

The truth is that the rest doesn't take care of itself. You need to consider "the rest of it" up front. Instead of going after a specific job title, start thinking about the environments in which you will thrive. Then find that right place. Turn the process around by first looking into your unique values and *then* finding a role and organization that speaks to you. You have to determine what your priorities and values are *before* you dive into a new job. No other person can decide for you what your value system is or what type of organization or company will be in alignment for you. You must put in the effort to find a strong fit.

Exercise 2: Values ❍

One great way to determine what you value most is to examine what you didn't like in your current or previous roles. Ask yourself what would have been better, if it weren't for "X"? Consider things like:

- the commute—How far would you really be willing to drive each day?
- the physical space/environment of the workplace—Are you comfortable in a cubicle? Do you like to work alone or along with others?
- the type of sector—Would you be most comfortable in a university, within the financial sector, in technology or healthcare, etc.?
- the organization's leadership
- the type of people that you want to work with—thinkers or feelers?
- the diversity of the workforce
- the potential for advancement and leadership roles
- the amount of travel
- the company's record of social responsibility and community engagement

Now flip that list around and create a list of what you *do* want to see in your next role:

1. *Deal-Breakers*

   This is your "must-have" list. For example: *Commute under 45 minutes*; *An organization promoting Green technology*; or, *No travel.*

2. *Compromises*

   The items that you are willing to compromise on based upon the quality of the opportunity.

3. *Can Waits*

   Things like promotion opportunities, bonuses, a new title, tuition reimbursement, etc. Whatever you're willing to wait for.

CAREER CONSTRUCTION

Career construction is another method to help you understand your career path. The framework was developed by Mark Savickas, Ph.D., and essentially helps to shine a beautiful light on the clues and common threads that exist within your life story. These vital bits of information help you discover a core theme in your personal holistic narrative that informs the next steps in your career path. What gives you meaning and purpose and how does that meaning and purpose relate to others? How are you of service to others? According to Savickas, the belief that what you do matters to others will help to bring focus to your identity and promote a sense of social meaning and relatedness.

Career construction ➊ helps you understand that many of the key projects and events in your life matter, both to yourself and as a positive ripple to other people. You'll key in on your personal theme by reflecting upon meaningful experiences from your life roles and see how they combine with your list of motivated skills. Then you'll align your theme with your current goals and future actions. This allows you to focus your energy and exploration on the types of roles (the work) and environments that are in alignment with your theme.

To help you learn more about yourself, you can reflect on your past to see and notice the patterns in your own personal narrative. What themes and patterns emerge in relation to your career? The point is not to determine your career through any types of codes or easy classifications; the point is to subjectively consider what your career narrative says about you and where you want to go in the future.

Exercise 3: Journey to the past

For this exercise, spend some time journaling about these two questions:

- What are three of your earliest recollections?
- Who did you admire when you were growing up (real or fictional)? List three heroes/role models

When you're done writing, review your answers. What patterns or trends can you link to your work or desired career? Where would you most like to go, based on your past? It would be ideal to complete a full career construction interview with a counselor or coach who is trained in this model.

FORMAL ASSESSMENTS

In judo, testing for the next belt is seen as an opportunity to demonstrate the capabilities, improved knowledge, and refined techniques you've accumulated. It's also an incentive to learn more and grow from the experience. Just like testing for that next belt in judo assess your knowledge and skills, a formal assessment can help you to understand more about yourself, like your personality preferences, character strengths, and current areas of interest. Keep in mind that an assessment is not an absolute; it's simply a tool to provide focused information to help you digest and apply to your process of exploration.

An assessment can be used at any stage of a career path, from career launch to mid-career transition. It can also be useful for those who are transitioning into pre or post-retirement careers. If you're in school, a career assessment may be used more stringently to help you identify what you want to major or minor in, as part of your plans for a degree. As a career is launched, or during growth stages of a career, assessment data can help you identify and leverage your strengths or match your interests to a sector or type of organizations you might want to work in. During a mid-career transition, however, you may not be as able, or as interested, in a full about-face on a career path. In that case, an assessment can be used to make smaller directional shifts, perhaps only a 45° or 90° change.

Here are two of the most commonly used and prominent assessments in use. Both of them have been taken by millions of people all over the world and can be understood and applied in many different arenas.

The Myers Briggs Type Indicator (MBTI)

This well established personality assessment is one of the oldest and most popular for a reason. For over 70 years, it's been continually updated and is used in multiple areas including career development, team-building, and couples counseling. The assessment provides a formal read on the patterns of how you use your mind, and dives into the ways in which you inquire, problem-solve, and view the world. The MBTI Career Report uses the common language of the assessment to look into 22 job *families*, or categories of related careers. It ranks the career families in which your specific personality type might thrive.

An MBTI assessment provides a general personality type denoted by four letters that together give you a framework of reference for both you and others. Each letter in the personality type reveals certain fundamental strengths. Your personality designation can help you to see how other people who share your personality type have found success and satisfaction in a career. For example, if you are an outgoing, creative, people oriented, spontaneous individual, in Myers Briggs language you'd be "ENFP" (Extroversion + Intuition + Feeling + Perceiving), and you might find happiness in a job that involves others and includes opportunities for change. Advertising, event planning, and physical therapy might be a great fit for you. Contrast this with to an ISTJ personality (Introversion + Sensing + Thinking + Judging) who might enjoy the more structured role of an accountant, computer programmer, or surgeon.

By asking you a series of questions, the MBTI helps you to determine several key factors about yourself. First, you learn where you fall on the spectrum of introvert to extrovert (I and E). You'll find out what most energizes you, ranging from quieter one-on one or small group activities to those with larger groups of people outside your personal environment. Second, the assessment helps you recognize how you process information: do you focus on the core data or do you like a "big picture" analysis (Sensing, S or Intuition, N)?

For decision-making, you'll discover if you look to logic (Thinking, T), or to what is best for the people involved (Feeling, F)?

Finally, you'll learn about your relationship to structure. Do you prefer schedules and lists to get things accomplished? Or do you need to be spontaneous and to stay open to new information (Judging, J) or (Perceiving, P)?

It's important to note that all types are equal; no one type is better than the other. Each has its unique attributes and challenges.

The MBTI can be helpful at any stage of your career ➊. The data and potential insight it provides can support a variety of career moves. Additionally, a professional who is trained in interpreting the feedback report can be of tremendous help to guide you through the results because, as many people who have taken an assessment well know, having a list of traits and preferences doesn't inform you how to translate the results for the real world. For example, your Myers Briggs "type" may point you to a career in mathematics. But interpretation, discussion, and exploration can guide you to more specific paths, such as math teacher or professor, sports statistician, mathematical modeling specialist, or actuary.

Working with a professional will allow you to explore the characteristics and strengths associated with each preference (letter), along with the combined four-letter personality code. By recognizing the qualities and patterns related to each letter and the complete four-letter code, you'll be more likely to find a better-fitting career.

The Strong Interest Inventory (SII)

This robust assessment (including 80 years of history and multiple updates) compares your interests to those reported by individuals of your gender in 130 occupational roles and across six theme codes. The benefit of this assessment is that you can immediately springboard into exploration mode for specific sectors and careers. Through a series of questions, the Inventory determines your highest correlations to each of the six themes: Realistic (R), Investigative (I), Artistic (A), Social (S), Enterprising (E), and Conventional (C), based upon pioneering work from the late psychologist John Holland, Ph.D. Dr. Holland proposed that "people search for environments that let them exercise their skills and abilities, express their attitudes and values, take on problems and roles they find stimulating and satisfying, and avoid chores or responsibilities they find distasteful or formidable." Once you determine these personality traits for yourself, then you can drill down into specific careers that may match your characteristics. For example, if you find that your theme code from the SII is EAS (Enterprising, Artistic, and Social), you can select eight to twelve job titles associated with the EAS theme (like chef, restaurateur, arts and entertainment manager, training and development specialist) that are of interest, and then drill down further into each of these.

As with the MBTI, getting the information in the reports to really serve you may require the help of a professional who is qualified to administer and explore the results of the assessment with you. A professional can help you discover the creative opportunities that match your interests. You may even find that you are already in a role that's a good fit for you; it's just that the environment isn't. In that case, the critical next steps will not be on *what* you will do, but on *where* to do your thing.

My client Alex is a great example of this. He had twelve years of experience as an accountant and was a lifelong resident of Atlanta, Georgia. He enjoyed being an accountant but he knew that something was missing. When he took the Strong Interest Inventory, his results showed a solid match with marine biology and marine science. I double-checked the results, convinced that they'd gotten mixed up somehow, but nope, they were correct. When I asked Alex about his interests, he responded, "Well, I've been volunteering at the Georgia Aquarium. I've really enjoyed assisting with the student programs and promoting community engagement. Plus all of the creatures and marine life are very cool."

After more discussion, I asked Alex if he'd ever considered becoming an accountant at the aquarium. His college degree was in accounting and he enjoyed doing the work of an accountant. Twelve years into his career, it was not very likely that Alex would embrace a major shift and invest in several more years of schooling to become a marine biologist, but he could pivot and move to a new environment in which his interests could be more fully realized. Alex already had the right fit career, but not the right environment.

An in-depth reading of an assessment can help you to discover alternative career roles and work settings. (See the Resources page at www.careerjudo.com for a list of websites to help you find applicable titles and roles in organizations.) ◑

Exercise 4: Occupations and settings of interest ❿

After taking the MBTI or SII assessment, or preferably both, highlight those occupations or settings that are of particular interest to you. Then, create a list of eight to twelve areas or career paths. An area can be either an organization or a role. For instance, in the case of the restaurant manager, it may be of interest to research both the title of restaurant manager, along with support roles— such as marketing, operations, finance, training, and purchasing—at a company that owns multiple high-end restaurants. The information on an interest inventory provides solid clues to distinct job titles, related "cousin" career paths, and potentially better fitting environments in which you can leverage your strengths.

MARKET RESEARCH: EXPLORING PROFILES OF PEOPLE IN YOUR TARGET ROLES

Judo invites us to cultivate a consciousness of our posture, balance, and movement while channeling our energy into the current exchange with our partner. A *judoka* must nurture his or her awareness to recognize when momentum and strategy meet that split-second opportunity to execute a technique with an opponent. In much the same way, the time and energy you dedicate to your career search and exploration will demand focus. Once you define your motivated skills, values, personality, and interests, you'll be able to narrow your focus by researching the roles and organizations that might be more in alignment with a career that fits you well.

Start by figuring out *who* is doing the kinds of things that you want do. For example, you can explore LinkedIn profiles and membership directories of professional associations to research people in your target roles. Do your best to uncover their academic backgrounds and the progression of their professional development and career. Find out where they work and review any profile information they have listed. You can also read books, magazines, trade journals, bios on company websites, and more, about the people in your target areas.

Then see if you can find out *how* they got to where they are now. Employ a variety of sources to help you understand what the career progression has been for people who are doing what you want to do. Whether you want to be a human resources specialist, a social media strategist, or an expert in environmental sustainability, find people who are doing what you want to do, and examine what they did to get there.

A useful tool in your research may be the U.S. Bureau of Labor Statistic's Occupational Outlook Handbook (it's online and free) where you can get the descriptions of an occupational role. Another tool, of course, is an internet search. Type '*Occupational Description for* _____' into your browser and see what you get.

Once you've gotten an overall view of the role, then it's time to dig deeper into the more subjective components of each role.

DEGREES OF SEPARATION

It's normal to reach a point in a job search where you exhaust the more obvious research ideas and run out of networking contacts. That's when it's time to start brainstorming about the types of organizations that might benefit from the scope and depth of your background. It's the time to start thinking *degrees of separation* from your current job title. For example, if job openings in your industry are disappearing, or perhaps you're experiencing some burnout in a traditional role, where do you turn? You can start by looking at the same career, but in an alternate environment or from a different perspective. For example a mechanical engineer might move from a job within a manufacturing organization to a role with a company that focuses on something entirely different, like product service and support, refurbished equipment, or green technologies.

To help you generate ideas for potential job titles using this approach, have discussions with professionals and others who know you, such as mentors, experienced colleagues, close friends, career coaches, and advisors and members within your alumni association or professional associations. Also, take advantage of available alumni career services to conduct Internet searches using the question, "What can I do with a major in_____?" Take advantage of resources that offer lists of job titles and environments that have a direct connection, are somewhat related to, or are outliers related to specific academic majors.

Exercise 5: Generating ideas for your next career role ❍

At this stage, it's beneficial to create a *hit list* of roles and organizations of interest to you. Rather than pushing forward, focus on diving a bit deeper to gather key information for each entry on your hit list. Then concentrate on answering the following questions for each role or organization that you've selected:

1. Is it a growing industry, has it leveled off, or is it dying? For instance, becoming a travel agent might seem like a great idea, but traditional travel agencies have gone the way of the dodo since people usually book travel for themselves online these days. Yet guided specialty travel tours and eco-travel adventures are on the rise.

2. What is the sector like? The work environment? Which professional organizations are representing and advancing this role? What educational and professional development is needed to be competitive and ultimately thrive in this role?

3. Make a list of pros and cons for each role. While this may seem a little academic, the exercise is subjective and tells you about yourself. You are filtering each pro or con through your own set of skills and strengths, values, personality preferences, and interests. Your perspectives and concerns will be unique to you. For instance, one person may love to have travel in their work schedule, while another may have children at home and consider extensive travel a "con." Do you like structure and hierarchy? Or do you prefer an environment that is flat: offering project teams rather than several levels of staff and management? Do you like working with thinking, analytical types of people, or feeling, people-centric types? Do you like wearing formal business attire for work or casual attire with your mobile office in a messenger bag?

4. Narrow down your list to four or five roles by looking at the roles realistically. Ask yourself, "Is this role viable for me at this point in my life?" For instance, now that you've seen that a marine biologist needs an additional 5-7 years of schooling for a Ph.D., are you willing to put in the time, effort, and additional money needed to pursue this role? Or perhaps a career in film production requires a move to New York City of Los Angeles. Are you prepared to make that move?

BRIDGING THE GAP

No matter how many times I step onto a judo mat, the feeling of the tatami under my bare feet always brings a rush of emotions. It's time to approach the edge of the mat, slip off my sandals, step forward onto the tatami, and execute a standing bow as a show of respect for the history, science, and art of judo. My pulse quickens with pride, exhilaration, camaraderie, and anxiety. These feelings are bundled with healthy doses of humility and trust as I work to become a more skilled martial artist.

In judo, we learn to turn our awareness inwards to discover our strengths and weaknesses, not with self-pity or self-criticism, but with compassion and an interest in forward growth and improvement. In Career Judo, you can use that same sense of humility and trust from the judo mat; you may not have the credentials necessary to move into a new role or industry just yet, however you can highlight those great skills that you *do* currently possess as you transition into a role that fits you.

Once you've completed your assessments and market research as described above, and you've narrowed down your list of viable roles, then you're ready to enter into the next stage of inquiry: digging deeper into the education, training, professional development, and credentials that are needed for these roles To do this, you can review live job postings on quality job boards and company web sites, as well as reach out to your network and ask if they know anyone in those roles. You can use credible sites like Linkedin.com, Glassdoor.com, TheMuse.com, and Indeed.com to search, using key words in the job title. You can also explore the *Careers/Employment* web pages at organizations of interest. To find these organizations, use a Book of Lists for your area, industry directories from the library, Chamber of Commerce directories, specialty lists from FastCompany.com, Fortune.com, Inc.com, GreatPlacestoWork. com, TheMuse.com, BestPlacestoWork.org, and lists of top companies in your city. A Google search for top places to work and your city name should pull up some useful resources.

Especially when you're launching a new career or transitioning into a new industry, you must look at the gap between what you have been doing and what you aspire to be doing and ask how you can bridge that gap. You might ask, "How can I be a viable candidate when my resume doesn't present a strong background for that particular area?" That's a legitimate concern, for which professional development is the answer. Seminars, workshops, conferences, credit or non-credit courses, MOOCs webinars, and independent reading or learning can all be done starting right now. Any type of learning and development that's related to your new area of choice can be a substantial benefit and can give new structure and energy to your career search.

Another area worth looking into is professional certification. Employers appreciate professional certifications because they show the decision-maker that a candidate has already put forth the energy and effort necessary for pursuing this specialty area, and is not waiting to be asked to move in a particular direction. By obtaining a certification, the candidate demonstrates that he or she is claiming an area of expertise and relevant knowledge; skills and experience have been validated by this certification. It's as if you're saying to potential employers: "Not only do I offer a solid background, but I've also obtained this professional credential and you can easily plug me into your organization. I'm ready to hit the ground running and bring value to your organization immediately. You won't have to invest a lot of time and money in additional training; I come to you with the necessary strengths in this specialty area."

How great does that sound? Even if you haven't yet achieved your certification but are pursuing it, you can mention on your resume and LinkedIn profile that you are currently pursuing that credential, and include your anticipated date of completion.

The specialized graduate certificate has been trending in academic circles and can be worthwhile for those looking to grow and specialize. It falls between the bachelor's and the master's degree and is usually 12 to 18 credit hours. This certificate can be a stepping-stone to a master's degree, or it can be a stand-alone credential. For instance, if you plan to concentrate on human resources or organizational development, then you may decide to do a graduate certificate in order to really dive in and specialize in that area. A graduate certificate helps to brand you as a specialist. With traditional on-campus classes, hybrid classes, or fully online programs available, you have incredible flexibility in obtaining these certificates.

The biggest consideration concerning academic credentials is whether the college or university is regionally accredited. Regional accreditation is the highest standard in the U.S., as opposed to national accreditation. There are six regional accrediting bodies in the U.S., and you need to make sure that if you pursue college coursework or an academic credential that any credits earned are transferable on a regional accreditation level. They represent the highest quality. There may also be an added layer of specialty accreditation for degree programs for professions like business, nursing, counseling, and education, in addition to regional accreditation.

Exercise 6: Identifying the gaps ○

Once you've identified your key target roles, look at the gaps that exist between your current role and those you desire to pursue. Write down the types of qualifications employers are asking for in job postings. What have you come across in your research that is necessary to function in the role? For each role, list out the gaps along with the corresponding skill or training. Then start doing some Internet research to identify potential development activities like seminars, workshops, and certifications, or academic certificate and degree programs that will allow you to fill this gap. Be completely honest with yourself: decide what steps will be truly viable for you, considering your current commitments and the cost and time that the education or training options might demand.

INFORMATIONAL INTERVIEWS

Whether you are just starting down the research path or have already started to network with others, you can dig deeper into the roles you've chosen with *informational interviewing*. This valuable meeting is simply a casual discussion that you set up with someone who is already working in the role you're exploring. Ideally, your interviewee can tell you about the good, the bad, and the ugly concerning their experience in that career role and setting. As you narrow down your list of potential roles for further consideration, the informational interview offers you a solid next step as you explore options. It is a great tool for gathering credible, real-world information about career roles and organizations of interest to you. Unfortunately, informational interviewing often prompts anxiety, even dread, in the job-seeker, perhaps almost as much as a job interview. It can be hard to "put yourself out there" and ask others for help in the job search, especially by asking people beyond friends and family to provide contacts or introductions. Yet approximately 70% of jobs are found, not through job boards, but through researching specific companies of interest, networking, and leveraging contacts. Which makes the informational interview a key component in the job search. Make no mistake, networking (of which informational interviews are a large part), is work; however, it can be motivating and can propel your career search forward.

In judo and martial arts, we look to conquer our fears by first identifying the fear (such as, "I'm afraid of being thrown"), and then practicing proven techniques that build confidence and reduce fear. We might ask ourselves, "What throws, holds, chokes, or arm bars can I practice that will limit the chance of being successfully attacked by my opponent? What fears do I have about being thrown and pinned to the mat?"

The same approach can be adopted in the career-search process. Identify the anxiety-producing fears you might have about conducting informational interviews. Procrastination can be a symptom of fear, so if you procrastinate, look deeper. Take a moment to write down all of the reasons that you don't feel that an informational interview is important. You might list things like, "People don't like to be bothered," or "I don't know anything about this industry and they'll think my questions are foolish," or "They don't know me, so why would they respond to my request?" or "I don't have a large enough network to find people."

How can you attack these concerns with well thought-out information and action?

Let's tackle some of the most common concerns. You may think that you only have a few limited professional contacts. But as with other parts of the career search, it helps to look outside of the traditional job "box" and include neighbors, acquaintances from your place of worship and your child's school, your hobbies, your sports teams, and those providing you with professional services like doctors, dentists, hygienists, chiropractors, massage therapists, lawyers, accountants, and hair stylists. Each of these people is typically connected to another 250 people or more (250 being the average number of "friends" on Facebook). And while it might feel awkward to reach out beyond friends and family about your job search, most people love to talk about themselves, their roles, their career path, and their organizations.

In the case of informational interviews, if you don't already know someone in the role or organization you're targeting, you'll want to send emails to friends and other network members, asking if they know anyone (who knows anyone, who knows anyone) working in the roles and organizations you're targeting. Ask if they would be willing to make a phone or email introduction. I would discourage you, though, from sending out a blanket email to everyone you know that you are "searching for a job and need help." Mass emails will likely become junk that no one reads or responds to. Be specific and selective with your requests, so the other party understands what you are asking for and how they may be able to help you.

You're not asking for a job

When you send a message to your contact, it should always be respectful, pleasant, and cognizant of their time. Make room in your schedule to meet when they are available and only meet for the length of time that you have agreed to, regardless of the conversation that arises. Ask for 30 to 60 minutes of their time, in a meeting for coffee, breakfast, or lunch, or whatever works best for their schedule. To frame the question, you might say something like:

> "[Name of initial contact] gave me your name. I'd like to learn about your experience as a _____, or your career path at _____ company. Do you have 30 minutes to meet over coffee? My treat."

If a face-to-face meeting is too complicated or not practical (they live four states away), then arrange a phone call to conduct the informational interview.

Do your best to focus on the fact that you're only setting up a friendly meeting to have a conversation and gather feedback. It's not an interview for a job. It might help to keep your nerves to a minimum and remove some of the squeamishness that people often have about asking others for help. If the person you meet happens to be impressed with your knowledge, personality, and background, then they may keep you in mind for a future opportunity, but that is not the purpose or the end goal of an informational interview.

Time and patience will be needed to find contacts and to schedule interviews with them. Like all parts of the strategic job search, you'll have to be tenacious. Once at the interview, the following questions might be helpful:

1. Why did you choose this path?
2. What are the best and worst aspects of your job?
3. Where do you want to go in your career?
4. What would you do differently?

5. Which professional organizations do you find helpful?

6. How do you keep current in your role?

Be friendly and professional with all those you meet for informational interviews. Respect their time and be sure to thank them for their insight and assistance. Also, be sure to send a handwritten thank-you note; it's a nice personal touch that makes a positive impact.

Exercise 7: Get the ball rolling - initiate an informational interviewing email or call to a starter list of five different contacts. Let them know that you are starting a job search and provide them with your top four to five roles or organizations of interest. Ask if they know anyone in those career roles or settings and whether they would be willing to set up an introduction for you. If nothing materializes, contact another four to five of your contacts. It can be very helpful to set up a spreadsheet listing the people you contacted, a date, the type of message you left, and any other information you'd want to know in the future about the call. ◑

JUMP ONTO THE JUDO MAT

Once you have identified profiles of people who are doing what you want to be doing, and you're actively looking at what training or development you need to start pursuing that specialty track or specialty certification, then your next step is to get out there.

As a young adult, I had the pleasure of attending a one-day training clinic with Jason Morris, an American silver medalist in judo at the 1992 Olympics. I had the distinct honor of being thrown around a judo mat by an Olympian! It was both an exciting and humbling experience. I would bow to Jason, grip the lapels of his *gi* and start gliding my feet along the mat, only to end up lying on the mat looking up at the ceiling of the dojo.

With each of my attempts to engage Jason, he would make quick work of my attack by countering with what seemed like an effortless technique fueled by speed and precision. As I lay on the ground, he extended his hand to help me get to my feet, displaying the grace of a seasoned student, competitor, and instructor.

In the world of judo, we engage in *randori*, practicing with like-minded individuals. In your pursuit of a career that fits you, you also need to engage with like-minded professionals, even if they are in a different place in their "training." You can go to meetings with people who are already on your desired path, hosted by professional associations and organizations. You'll need to rub elbows and chat with people who are doing what you want to be doing. Look into national memberships and regional or state memberships in order to find the people who represent your area of specialty interest. Research and recognize the value of Meetup groups, formal events, lunch and learns, seminars, conventions, and webinars; consider them an essential part of finding your better fit career.

Exercise 8: Research groups ◑

Research a few groups or Meetups that you can attend over the next month and schedule them in your calendar. Make a commitment to yourself to attend the events, even if you must attend alone. Remember that, just like an informational interview, you are only representing yourself, not your job search. Just be friendly and focus on being your authentic self. Ask others about their career journey and professional interests; it will make you memorable.

CHAPTER 2: YELLOW BELT

CLAIMING AND PROMOTING YOUR BRAND

"The privilege of a lifetime is to become who you truly are."
— Carl G. Jung

EMBRACING YOUR UNIQUENESS

A popular misconception about judo and other martial arts is that becoming a master is all about learning some necessary techniques. But there's more to it than that. The setup—the strategic steps and movements that you execute just prior to the moment of attack—is equally as important to a successful win on the mat, if not more so. With a strong set-up, a judoka can win a match with the most basic techniques.

In the same way, finding a well-fitting career isn't about trying to learn the ultimate techniques or skills necessary to morph yourself into a predetermined role. Instead, it's about discovering more about yourself and then finding that role or organization that aligns with your skills and strengths, values, personality, and interests. Once you've defined that target role, you can start to market yourself purposefully and get recognized by potential employers who are offering that role. We call this *personal marketing*. It's helpful to approach the concept of personal marketing not from an egoistic standpoint— with an attitude of "I'm smart and talented and I deserve this role"—but with the mindset of "What development activity and accomplishments will put me in a positive light, help me stand out from the crowd, and get noticed?"

You may have heard the quote from Dr. Seuss: "Why fit in when you were born to stand out?" The quote is sometimes accompanied by a picture of a herd of regular zebras and one stand-out rainbow-striped zebra. You want to present yourself to be that zebra with the rainbow stripes during your job search. Personal marketing isn't about presenting your skills, experience, and accomplishments in the same old way so that they look like everyone else's. It's about showing your personality and skills in a dynamic and tangible way in order to catch the eye of a potential new employer.

BECOMING AN EXPERT

On the judo mat, there are no pretenses. Efforts to pretend to be a master of all skills and faking moves you haven't yet grasped will quickly land you on your back. In Career Judo, the principle still applies: you don't need to be a master of all skills, only a master of those that are most important for your target roles. When you look at job postings and descriptions, it might be easy to assume that an organization expects you to be a master of everything. But keep in mind that a job posting is really more like a Christmas list or a wish list. A recruiter or hiring manager is putting everything they desire from a "perfect" candidate into a particular job listing so they can see how close the candidates come to their ideal profile. It may seem that employers want a generalist in the role, but truly what they value is a specialist: someone who can provide unique value and mastery of a role or function. Like any area of the business, employers are looking for a return on their investment and they want to know that their investment in you is going to be worthwhile. Directly or indirectly, an employer is always asking: "What can you bring to my organization that is unique and that allows me to put you into a specific role on a specific team, where you will bring immediate value to my organization?"

You may think that you don't necessarily have the polished skills, mastery of a certain subject, or expertise for a specific role. But when you look at moving on in your career or becoming more of a specialist and authority on the matter, then you have to start claiming and embracing your area of expertise. It's a time to step out onto the judo mat with heightened awareness, with confidence in the techniques you've practiced, and with the wisdom that comes from trial, error, and success.

You can embrace one to three competencies that fit you the best; they are the ones that demonstrate the motivated skills that you enjoy using and the fit where you feel connected and do your best work. For example, if you feel energized and engaged when you are training a peer on a new process, you might want to seek a role as a corporate trainer or project manager with a company that specializes in delivering training products and services. You can analyze the gaps in your background by comparing live job postings to your experience and skills in your resume and asking yourself questions like:

Are you lacking project management (PM) training?

Is a master's degree a core requirement?

Do you need to earn a certification for the corporate training or PM sectors?

Do you need training on a specific software product?

What is keeping your professional profile from being recognized as a strong fit for this type of career role?

Then focus your attention on what's next: nurturing your professional development, seeking additional education, or learning more through your own reading and practice, workshops or formal college coursework in the areas that suit you best. All of these activities will help to brand you as a budding specialist.

Are you wearing too many hats?

You may have discovered that in your zeal to be all things to all people and to fit into a variety of roles that you really don't have an expertise in any one area. You might have allowed yourself to become watered down. Now's the time to courageously claim your area of specialization and promote your personal brand. That's why it's important to examine your values, stay true to them, and focus on your strengths for specific roles as you continue to grow and evolve.

For many job-seekers, wrapped within a fear of claiming to be an expert in something lies an unwillingness to let go of many of the hats that they've worn in the past. So they may wind up cheating themselves out of some opportunities that come their way. You may have learned to excel at many things and you've acquired many transferable skills; perhaps you've forced yourself to be good at something because it was critical to your current position. While some responsibilities may have been enjoyable, and others may not have been, you learned to do those dull and mundane tasks and continued to take them on as part of your job.

I'm not asking you to ignore and dump the transferrable skills; they will always be a part of you. You can still use those skills and even list them on your resume. However, you don't want to do them every day or every week. I'm proposing that you put each transferrable skill on the shelf like a hat, and, instead, highlight the motivated skills that you *do* want to use on an ongoing basis.

Letting go of your old hats might be difficult, since you want to be seen as a viable candidate for the roles represented by the entire wish list in the job postings you're reviewing. Yet you may be unknowingly allowing fear to create a subconscious fog that blocks your focus. For instance, you might think: "If I claim expertise in one or two areas, will I be eliminated from the other areas of consideration?" The answer is Yes. Absolutely. But those *other* areas of consideration won't be the strongest fit for you.

If you've already done the work to identify your motivated skills, completed a personality assessment, uncovered your unique interests, and defined the key elements that you want in a role, then you know which areas you want to concentrate on.

It's difficult to back away from the fear that you won't get an interview for a certain job, especially when that job is one that you find quite comfortable. However, once you define your area of specialization, you'll notice that your more narrow focus gives you more power to open more intriguing doors in your career search. Employers want to hear that you're excited about accounting in a particular sector, for example, or research and development, or that you are a power user of a core software product. Claiming a specialization allows you to more effectively hone in on the particular resources, networking opportunities, and learning experiences that are most aligned with the specialty. For instance, a business analyst will engage with peers and experts in very different conferences and networking groups than an accountant. You'll be able to more clearly define where your energy and time are best spent.

Best of all, once you claim your uniqueness, then you don't have to worry about all of the other areas that don't match or don't feel comfortable. You don't have to worry about representing those other skill sets that an employer has asked for, because you know that you can prove your expertise in a specific area or arena. It takes strength of will and determination to claim that "I will be true to myself and I will follow a particular strategy to go after the career goals that represent a best fit for me." But that is the path to finding the career that most aligns with who you truly are.

With this approach, you don't have to try to morph into a job title or show up on your first day of work with the thought, "Who do they expect me to be?" Instead, you can approach your career path from a position of strength, believing and achieving the awareness of, "This is who I want to be." You can make the choice to seek out the organization or role that best suits you and then claim that role. The Japanese call this awareness *zanshin* and in judo we give out a shout of energy (*kiai*) as we explode with focus and purpose.

A holistic view

Like everything else in your strategic job search, you'll want to look at personal marketing from a holistic viewpoint. By that I mean that you should review the entire range of your engagement in the world, including volunteer work, community involvement, advocacy work, hobbies, and interests as possibilities to highlight in your marketing. Are you passionate about particular political issues, human rights issues, animal rights issues, or the environment? All of these interests can potentially be shared in your personal marketing materials like resumes, letters, LinkedIn profiles, and so forth.

You should also expound on your professional development and training in your marketing. What workshops, seminars, conventions, courses, or lectures have you attended in the community or through professional networks and associations? Participation in workshops and other professional development can be a wonderful way to demonstrate that you are setting yourself apart and diving into a particular sector or specialization. You may have a solid academic background, however recruiters and hiring managers also like to see that you are now engaging in professional development and enhancing your knowledge and skills to gain expertise in a particular area.

Of course, you still want to promote your academic path by listing things like academic credentials, major and minor concentrations, certificates, honors programs, and others. Start thinking about all of your learning and development activities since completing your most recent academic program. These are key elements that will help to define you as different and unique, compared to your competition.

Exercise 9: Your Uniqueness

Do you know what makes you unique? List all of the workshops, certificates, academic credentials, programs, reading, networking, advocacy, and interests in your life. Now, narrow the list down to those that would bolster the specific area of expertise that you're targeting. Keep this list as a bold reminder of your distinctive life experiences to date. Remember, you don't really want to be seen as just another qualified job applicant, but rather as *the* applicant that stands out with a high quality profile.

RESUME BRANDING: WRITING YOUR PERFECT RESUME

Many people find themselves in search of that elusive creature known as the *perfect resume*. But there's a principle in judo called *tai sabaki* (body shifting) that can give you a more empowering perspective. Tai sabaki refers to the way in which a judoka changes his or her body position and orientation when executing a technique or being on the receiving end of one. As you write or update your resume, keep this idea in the back of your mind. You want to be flexible and be able to easily change your presentation in order to build and promote your number one brand: YOU. Create a strong, clear, and precise profile of someone who is gaining expertise or becoming a specialist in a particular area. It is wise to shift and refine the core focus of your brand by consistently updating your resume any time you complete meaningful professional growth and achieve milestones.

What is my brand?

If you run out of toothpaste, you decide to take a trip to the grocery store to pick some up. But when you get to that aisle in the store, you're faced with so many different kinds of toothpaste. As you gaze at the rows of brightly colored, shimmering boxes, you may not remember which toothpaste you like best, so you start trying to picture your brand of toothpaste. But why is this your go-to brand of toothpaste? What do you know about that brand? Does it have the freshest minty taste? Is it the best for fighting plaque and whitening? Is it natural and free of chemicals? How did the company convince you to purchase it?

When it comes to your resume, follow the same thought process. Like the *just right* tube of special toothpaste, you brand yourself as unique and special. What do you want people to know about you? What is it about you that is different and what can you uniquely offer an organization? How could you prompt an employer to choose you and call you in for an interview? How could you persuade an organization to call you back after the first interview? Once you have those answers, then that's the brand that you want to promote.

Branding titles

Branding titles can be professional titles or functional areas, depending upon which works better for your purposes. They represent roles that you have served in, roles that you are prepared to assume, or functional areas that represent your expertise, such as *Communications Manager* (title) or *Communications and Branding (a*reas). Decide what fits you best; for example, you could use "Social Media Strategy" (an area) instead of "Social Media Strategist" (a title). However, choose to show either areas or titles, not a mix of the two. Branding titles should express the core of what you choose to promote to a potential employer. You'll want to add two to three branding titles to the top of your resume, under your name, as well as on your LinkedIn profile and networking cards.

For someone who's in transition or just launching a career, it's best to use functional areas instead of titles. The use of functional areas give you a little bit more wiggle room in order to go after positions that you believe you are qualified for, without actually claiming that you have held a specific title previously.

Your professional profile

After you list your branding titles in your resume, add a professional profile section. You want to present impactful facts about your background, your uniqueness, and what you offer. Again, you want to stand out and distinguish yourself from others. It helps to add variety to your words, too. Instead of saying, "experience as a public relations professional," try "innovative and resourceful." Become comfortable using the thesaurus; it's a great way to describe yourself more effectively so you stand out.

There are a variety of ways to conclude your professional profile. For example, you could say, "My professional credentials include" or, "My academic credentials include" or, "My academic background and professional credentials include." I like to end the professional profile section with: *My full profile can be viewed on (insert LinkedIn profile URL).* This allows someone reading a digital version of your resume, with Internet access, to immediately click on the URL.

Anthony M. Stevens

Communications & Journalism ~ Social Media Strategy ~ Public Relations & Promotions

Atlanta, GA 30307 ▪ 404.566.7788 ▪ anthonyM@gmail.com

PROFESSIONAL PROFILE

Innovative and resourceful public relations professional experienced in communications, publicity, promotions, and social media; possess strong communication and interpersonal skills; well-organized with a strong attention to detail and exceptional ability to manage multiple projects under deadlines; team contributor with the motivation and experience necessary to advance program initiatives while supporting the organizations key objectives for growth and development. Full profile can be viewed at www.linkedin.com/in/anthonymstevens.

Core Strengths and Areas of Expertise Include:

- Communications Strategy
- Program & Campaign Development
- Publicity & Promotions
- Public Speaking & Engagement

- Social Media Strategy
- Creative/Dynamic Design
- Adobe Creative Suite
- Proofreading & Copy Editing

- Superior Client Relations
- Creative Thinking & Research
- Advancing Program Initiatives
- Deadline Driven

Sample resume heading and profile.

Hard skills

As you can see in the example, next up on your resume should be six to twelve bulleted hard skills (listed under "Core Strengths and Areas of Expertise"). These are skills that you believe that you can offer and that reinforce your branding. And where do you find this terminology? Right in the job postings. It's really effective to tailor your resume to a specific job and to use similar wording and labels as the recruiter has used in the job description (without copying exactly, of course). If you find several job postings that are very interesting to you, then print them out and go through them with a red pen or highlighter and identify the words or phrases that employers are using to target the hard skills you are trying to promote. You'll most likely see a lot of repetition among multiple job postings. If you see these types of skills repeated, then you'll know that these strengths are important for that role or sector.

You want to list hard skills because you don't want to promote empty or fluffy terminology. Phrases like "good communicator" or "good with people" are empty, trite, and overused. Instead of saying "good communicator," you can say, "communications strategy," "publicity" and "promotions," for example. Likewise, instead of saying "good with people," you can present, "coaching," "counseling," and "excels at conflict resolution."

As a general rule, it's best to stick to a chronological resume rather than a functional format. You may be tempted to use a functional resume because it seems to make sense and does have logic, but don't be fooled into thinking that the functional resume will hide gaps and transitions. Go with transparency and explain any gaps or transitions. Recruiters and hiring managers don't like to piece together the details from a functional resume; they prefer chronology.

Exercise 10: Resume building ◑

Now it's time to start building your resume! Start by thinking about what makes you stand out from the crowd and then use the resume building tips and examples from the resources page on the website.

THE PROCARD

A very simple, low cost, yet highly effective marketing tool is something that I call the *ProCard*. It is essential for your job search and for the professional networking that you'll do. If you already have your resume, then you'll know the two to three branding titles that you'll need for your *ProCard*.

To get your ProCards, go online and find a site to order high quality, low cost business cards, such as Vistaprint.com. Select a card template that is professional and pleasing to the eye and insert your content into the template. Remember the "KISS" rule about keeping it simple. Insert your name and any academic or professional credentials (*Andrew J. Smith, MBA, CPA*). Then insert two to three branding titles under your name

(*Accounting Leadership ~ Financial Management ~ Policy and Compliance*). Next, add your Linkedin vanity URL to the card (*www.Linkedin.com/in/ AJSmithMBA*). Finish the card by adding one (best) phone number and the email address you'll be using for your job search. You may find that creating a new, free email address/account for your job search can help you effectively sort through your daily volume of email messages.

You're done! Order your cards and when they arrive you are ready to go. Your *ProCard* is now a short cut to the resume content and profile you are promoting on Linkedin. It's like a resume in your pocket! Hand your *ProCard* out at meetings and networking events; to friends, family and colleagues; at interviews. Hand it out wherever the opportunity presents itself to promote yourself and to give people an immediate link to your resume content.

Exercise 11: Branding titles and areas ◑

If you haven't already done so, sit down and come up with a list of branding titles for yourself. Use the lists on the resources page for help. Then, go ahead and build your ProCard via any online printing resource that offers free templates and reasonably priced business cards.

THE COVER LETTER

Forget the drab, one-size-fits-all cover letters that you've used in the past. And also ignore the cover letter samples provided by publications and web sites that go on and on, paragraph after paragraph, essentially providing a condensed version of your resume. The former is too generic and the latter contains far too much information. These types of cover letters are not effective because the people you want to read them, like internal and external recruiters and hiring managers, *don't have the time to read a dense story.*

Remember that, like a resume, a cover letter is a business document, and a key rule for business documents is to keep the writing concise. So get directly to the point. If the resume itself only gets seven to ten seconds of attention from the reader on first glance, then the cover letter easily gets less. But a cover letter is often still requested by employers, so make sure that it is on point and delivers a message with impact.

So how do you construct a top-notch cover letter? By putting some "FEVER" in your letter!

F – FOCUS

Craft a document that clearly focuses on the type of opportunity, including associated titles, that you are qualified to assume. Don't leave the impression that you'll consider a variety of positions within the organization. There is a very real risk in stating that you are willing to be a manager, an analyst, or a project leader, or whatever they need you to be at this time. The reader is likely to conclude that your flexibility represents a lack of clarity regarding your strengths and experience.

E – EMPHASIZE

Emphasize why you believe that you will be a strong fit for the position, the team, and the organization. Do your homework and learn about the employer's culture, environment, structure, and work dynamics.

V – VALUE

Provide the prospective employer with a clear sense of the immediate value that you would bring to the organization.

Your letter should answer the question, *"Why should I consider you for this position?"*

E – EXPERTISE

Interject several bullet points to solidify in the reader's mind the expertise that you offer. Don't regurgitate all the bullets from your resume. Instead, include select words or phrases to express some of the hard skills, core strengths, and expertise you hold. These should align with the qualifications for the position you are seeking.

R – REQUEST

Close your letter with a strong request for a personal interview at the reader's convenience. Convey that you are ready to answer targeted questions and explain your background in detail.

If you invest the time and effort into crafting your cover letter with FEVER, you send the message that you are a professional who is focused, efficient, and serious about the position you are seeking.

LETTER OF INTRODUCTION

A cover letter is actually two letters in one. By simply changing the opening sentence, the document becomes a letter of introduction that is used to capitalize on your networking activities. The traditional cover letter often opens with something like "I am responding to your advertised opening for a [insert title, such as 'business analyst.']" A letter of introduction can open with something more like: "I spoke with Ellen Gates at a recent networking meeting for the Southeast Association of Business Innovation and she mentioned that your organization may be in need of a business analyst." The remainder of the letter can be your core cover letter, slightly edited to point out the specific value and expertise you would offer.

Customize all letters with the names and addresses of recipients and employers; this shows you put in a bit of effort. If you can't identify a specific person as the addressee for the letter, you can list *Human Resources Department* in the inside address and *Ladies and Gentlemen* as the salutation (not: *To Whom It May Concern*). Check and double-check the letter for grammar, spelling, and punctuation.

Exercise 12: Getting started on your cover letter ➊

Writing a great cover letter can be one of the most challenging aspects of the job search for many people, but what's even harder might just be getting started. If you already have a specific job or role in mind, begin crafting your cover letter using the process outlined above. If you don't have a specific role in mind, go ahead and begin a letter that describes all of the reasons why you would be a valuable addition to any company or organization. If you have networked recently, you can instead turn it into a letter of introduction.

REFERENCE SHEET

References do not belong on a resume, so you'll want to craft a separate document to present three to five of your professional references. Open the document with your heading (name, phone, email, optional physical address) and the title 'PROFESSIONAL REFERENCES.' Ideally a reference should be someone who has supervised your work. If you're a recent graduate, you can list one or two professors from your academic program. Peers at your places of employment and program managers at volunteer and community organizations can also be listed as references. The format of each reference entry on your document is pretty straightforward:

- Name of reference
- Their career title
- Their employer
- Snail mail address
- Best phone number
- Email
- A brief sentence about how you are connected to the individual. For example, *"Mr. Roberts served as my immediate supervisor during my four year tenure at JEL Industries, Inc.).*

Exercise 13: Creating your reference sheet ❶

Following the process outlined above, create your reference sheet. Unlike your cover letter, it shouldn't change much throughout your job search. Be sure to ask each individual for permission before you list them as a reference.

THE ELEVATOR SPEECH

Judo and other martial arts emphasize the need to remain flexible so you can apply different skills to different situations. As you search for the career that fits you well, you can learn how to build and use another tool —the *elevator speech*—to your advantage in all types of networking situations. It helps you to continually engage with the people in your environment, armed with a focused message.

You may or may not already be familiar with elevator speeches, depending upon where you are in your career search. No matter what, you need to master yours and be ready to use it at any time. Students can benefit from having an elevator speech, too, to use in interviews for scholarships, internships, grad school, and coops.

The elevator speech helps to set you apart from others by keying in on your uniqueness. It's the chameleon of career resources since you adapt it to the setting you're in. It effectively and succinctly provides a response to the prompt, "Tell me a little bit about yourself." The need to have a well thought out response may come up in a seminar or a workshop, at networking events, or as an opener in an interview for an internship or job. Having a prepared, focused, and concise reply can be incredibly helpful to your job search.

First, you'll develop an elevator speech to commit to memory. Then you'll adapt it, on-the-fly, to fit the situation that you find yourself in. As always with Career Judo, you want to look at your elevator speech more holistically so that you share many aspects about yourself; it's not just a simple recitation of your resume. Some career professionals advise that an elevator speech should be all about your professional life or academic life. However, I firmly believe that the employer's perspective is this: *I'm hiring a human being and I want to know more about this individual.*

So often when a career seeker is asked about herself, the answer she gives the employer is something like, "I'm an entry-level junior analyst and I have a degree in business administration. I'm focusing my career on this area of development and I want to be a senior business analyst." But, if you'll notice, the request is not "Tell me about your career," or "Tell me about your work," or even "Tell me about your academic path." The prompt is: "Tell me about *yourself.*" It pays to respond to that request specifically.

Here's the trick. It's best to deliver your reply to such a request within a 30- to 60-second window. That makes it doubly important not to focus only on one particular aspect of your career. Start with your name, mention where you're from (particularly if you are a non-native to a particular area), and perhaps say a little bit about your childhood or family background, especially if there's something interesting there. You're looking for something that sets you apart in a nice way.

You could then tell the listener what sparked your interest in the field or role that you're pursuing. Or you could refer to the time or event in your background that really made you think about pursuing a particular path—whether that's becoming a veterinarian, or becoming a teacher, or becoming an accountant, what sparked that interest? Were you the kid who was constantly taking the toaster apart and that led to your interest in engineering? Did you always build houses for birds and turtles and that led to your architecture degree?

Also consider including a few words about your educational path. Why did you choose your particular degree? Did you add a minor, a concentration, or a certification? Did you do something different at college, like being a member of the University political stage? Did you study abroad, do any internships, or participate in the Student Council, the theater, groups, or a sports team? Give your listener something unique and different to learn about you.

Next, you may want to talk about your career progression, but again, this should not dominate the elevator speech. Sprinkle in a few highlights or stepping-stones to let people know what you've achieved to date and that you are pursuing goals. You might include mention of your professional development, a specialized training, or the pursuit of a certain certification. Employers are interested in hearing that you are working towards enhancing your credentials and therefore your specialty knowledge and skills. In some cases you may even want to speak of the target role or goal that you're going after.

With each element of the elevator speech, try to include what makes you memorable and helps you stand out when compared to the 20 other people that a hiring manager or decision-maker has talked to that day. I've been known to mention in my elevator speech that I am a black belt in judo; that I worked out with an Olympic medalist who threw me all over the mat; and that I loved every minute of it. An interesting fact of your own sets you apart from the competition and helps people to remember you.

When you're trying to figure out what makes you unique, it's helpful to go back to your list of motivated skills. They are the ones you really enjoy and you really want to build upon and leverage as much as possible on a daily basis. The motivated skills can point towards things that you would want to highlight within your elevator speech.

When you think about all of the components of your elevator speech, it seems like a lot, but the time it takes to deliver it needs to be less than one minute. You'll also want to adapt it to each situation you find yourself in. To make it easier for you to use it on the spur of the moment, make sure you are clear about which are the core elements— those that absolutely need to be communicated. The speech you give for a job interview may be a bit longer than the one you say to someone you meet at a seminar or community event. Practice your elevator speech a lot to memorize it, both alone and with a partner. That will help ensure that it doesn't come across as rote or rehearsed, and that it has flow and style. Feel free to take a look at my elevator speech on my website at www.careerjudo.com.

Exercise 14: Building your elevator speech ❶

Use the list below to help get you started. Build a sentence or two around each one and write them down.

- Name
- I'm from…
- Childhood/family fact
- What sparked my interest in the field or role
- Education
- Hobbies and community engagement
- Career progression

- Professional development and specialized training
- Target role
- Additional interesting fact

Once you have the speech written down, practice it a few times in the mirror. After you are able to confidently deliver the speech without looking at your notes, ask a partner or friend for help. Ask for honest feedback, such as places where you may want to strengthen or buffer. It might help for them to read this section of the book over first in order to get a sense of what's needed.

LINKEDIN: DEVELOPING A SOCIAL MEDIA PROFILE THAT GETS NOTICED

How do you get noticed in your job search? In the past, people crafted a lengthy cover letter to tell their career story and coupled it with a generic, one-size-fits-all resume. But nowadays, a targeted career search is very different than that. You are building a package of information, including a focused resume that conveys your value, a list of select professional references, a simple, targeted cover letter, and—incredibly important in today's world—a LinkedIn profile ❐.

Many people have reservations about creating or enhancing a profile on LinkedIn. You may be reluctant to put yourself out on the web, uneasy with the strength of LinkedIn's security or privacy efforts, or intimidated by the technology and process of learning the social media application. Or you might feel that you don't know what to showcase about yourself. But LinkedIn is not only a valuable networking and job search platform; it has become a necessary tool for career development.

LinkedIn is the world's largest professional social media and its value lies in its ability to help you find connections to people and organizations. Through friends and family already on LinkedIn, it allows you to seek out possible links to decision makers and professionals in target organizations. It can also provide recommendations and an encapsulated resume to those who are seeking your unique skills.

Most importantly, though, an online presence is more valuable than ever, and LinkedIn is quite possibly the first place a potential employer will look online when receiving your resume. This means that your LinkedIn profile must have more scope and depth than your resume and it must also satisfy your potential employer's curiosity to learn about your academic background and professional journey. It might help to think of the resume as the Cliff notes and your LinkedIn profile as the book.

In addition to providing a state of the art platform for your professional profile, LinkedIn provides opportunities to:

- create and advance a brand
- offer links to multimedia content and work samples
- promote the quality of completed projects
- join and contribute to groups of interest
- research organizations of interest
- search available jobs
- store an ever-growing network of colleagues, peers, and individuals sharing a like mindset

Rather than shy away from LinkedIn, I highly recommend that you tame the beast by engaging in learning activities instead. Read web content and books from Amazon about how to get the most out of LinkedIn. Watch online tutorials. Take a class in your community (through high school adult education, college continuing education, classes at a community center or place of worship, etc.) using the free learning resources at LinkedIn. Ask a friend or co-worker who is currently on LinkedIn for some assistance in building your profile. Engage professional help from a career coach or resume writer who offers LinkedIn writing services. Get proactive by creating, building, and grooming your presence on LinkedIn. Get yourself in a position to leverage the power of this essential career management tool.

Of course, as with all aspects of the branding of YOU, you want to emphasize your uniqueness. Especially on LinkedIn, an eye-catching and distinctive profile is a must. Here are a few easy steps to setting up an individualized LinkedIn profile:

1. Establish a free account with LinkedIn.com. The free account has so many bells and whistles that you don't need to start with a paid membership.

2. Don't reinvent the wheel. Simply migrate the content from your resume over to the particular sections of your LinkedIn profile.

3. Add a current professional (or "business casual") headshot to link your face with your content.

4. Pay very close attention to the information in the box at the top of your profile containing your photo and "Highlights" — it is what people see most:

   • **Headline**—This is your tagline. At first, LinkedIn automatically fills this field with the most recent position you've listed in the "Experience" section of your profile, but you can change it. Think of your headline as a personal slogan and as a set of search keywords. Include keywords and phrases that are related to your desired industry or profession so that when LinkedIn users enter those words in a search, you will more likely appear in the results. Even if you're still a student, you can get started building your profile; your headline can communicate your passion for your major.

   • **Location and Industry**—LinkedIn users can select their location and industry in these fields. It is a good idea to choose the industry you intend to enter and, if seeking a specific location for work, to choose that location for your profile. This way, you will appear in searches for that geographic area.

- **Public Profile URL**—LinkedIn allows you to create a vanity URL, to incorporate your name into the web address for your account, rather than a random alphanumeric string. Be sure to put this vanity URL on your ProCard and in your resume profile; it will give people immediate access to the focused resume content that you have used to build and maintain your LinkedIn profile.

5. Be sure to use your branding titles (described earlier in this chapter) under your name at the top of your LinkedIn profile.

6. Develop a strong yet concise narrative—a version of your elevator speech—to introduce your profile summary and to provide focus on the career role that you are pursuing.

7. List 8-12 bulleted strengths or areas of expertise within your Summary. Add them right under your narrative statement, as an element of your summary. These concise key terms and phrases should be pulled directly from the "Profile" or "Summary of Qualifications" section of your resume.

8. Enter your career experience into the LinkedIn account, listing your current or most recent position first. Focus on presenting strong descriptions of your contributions and accomplishments with each employer rather than filling it with a boring list of your job duties. Use LinkedIn's Media feature to add photos, PDFs, links to websites, and more, to demonstrate the strength and quality of your background.

9. Seek out credible recommendations from peers, references, instructors, mentors, and clients. When possible, offer short, solid recommendations in return, limiting them to only 2-4 sentences. When asking for a recommendation, request that the individual comment on one of your specific strengths. As a result, you'll have a number of recommendations on a variety of different strengths.

10. Search for groups on LinkedIn. There are thousands of groups available, so when you're searching, consider your career experience, academic background, community interest or volunteerism, and current interests. Group participation gives you the ability to start expanding your network immediately. Post interesting content (from online magazines, professional associations, blogs, etc.) to key groups once every 5-10 days to contribute and show that you're being present, mindful, and contributing to the group.

11. Take advantage of the many add-ons that are available to enhance your profile including media, projects, languages you speak, causes you care about, courses you teach, courses you've taken, and so on.) Use the Media feature to showcase your work samples, presentations, projects, and assignments. Always keep people informed on your current professional activities. You can also use status updates to notify others of blog posts you've posted recently, articles in your targeted area you have read lately and found interesting, a question you have about the field of interest, or a new success story from a job or internship.

12. Like a spider that builds and expands her web, continue to seek out, contact, and connect with professionals who are interested in networking and grow your own personal web. The hidden value in e-networking is in your ability to reach out and establish second and third tier connections, or more. Your network can include:

- Family members
- Friends and fellow students
- Internship or job supervisors and co-workers
- Professors, advisers, coaches, and former teachers
- People in volunteer and community groups, as well as those who share your hobbies
- Family friends
- And all of *their* connections

CHAPTER 3: GREEN BELT

THE PRO-ACTIVE JOB SEARCH

"It's time to start living the life you've imagined."
— Henry James

A s I continued to advance through the junior ranks in Judo, my sensei called upon me more and more to help him as he taught the children in the judo classes. I felt quite proud to have earned the trust of my sensei and I felt lucky to have been given the opportunity to teach the martial art I had grown to love. Eventually, I was promoted to Junior Instructor and led groups of students 5-12 years of age through demonstrations and practice of fundamental techniques. A few decades later, I stepped into the role of sensei myself, in a judo club in southwest Florida, where I taught adult judo classes as a black belt. These experiences may well have been the seeds of my desire to become an instructor in higher education. Like my early sensei, Professor George Strong, I received a graduate degree in Psychology and now teach undergraduate courses in psychology and human services. Teaching judo served as very practical experience for my career roles in professional coaching and higher education.

Most of us who practice martial arts always want to improve our skills no matter where we are in our practice or what belt level we've achieved. We do so by identifying what it takes to reach a certain goal, and then we break down that goal into its component parts. For instance, if a judoka wanted to master a more effective throw, she'd deconstruct the art of the perfect throw into its individual movements and then practice different aspects of that movement, like speed, balance, and timing.

In the dojo of life, if your goal is to land a job that fits you well, then you could break that goal down into smaller, more manageable steps—like focused networking and exploring targeted resources. Most of us have been lulled into thinking that all we need to do is to jump onto job boards like Indeed.com. But the truth is that a job board is only one small part of the targeted job search; it is only one step towards your goal.

Think of your job search like swaths of colors on a painting. Instead of employing just one method—like job boards—use a variety of tracks. Paint many different swaths to cover more of your canvas. For instance, if you're looking at job boards, add in networking, researching companies of interest, and looking into select industry resources, then each time you add one of these tracks (swaths of color), you add more breadth to the search, increasing your chances of finding a better fitting job.

NETWORKING TO PROMOTE YOUR BRAND

Many people feel that networking is one of the scariest and toughest ways to land a job. Many wonder, "Where should I network? How do I network? What will I do if they say No?" Most would rather hunt and peck through online job boards instead. Yet networking remains one of the top ways to find a job, and for good reason: more than 60% of people looking for work find it through connections. I tell all of my clients that it's the one track that they must engage in. (Cue the moans and groans!)

Let's make the dreaded word "networking" a little less scary by looking at it more closely. Networking starts with your phone. Scroll through the contacts in your cell phone and your email; this is where your networking begins. Start a list of all of your friends, family, colleagues, peers, club members, and people in your professional associations. Once you have that list, refine it further. Who are the potential rainmakers in your existing network? Who has a strong scope of connections and influence? You'll know who they are: they're the ones who are often trying to connect you with others.

Malcolm Gladwell called these people "connectors" in his book, *The Tipping Point,* while others may refer to them as *Rain Makers.* Start with these people, of course, but remember that everyone you know has connections and shouldn't be overlooked. You never know who or what another person may know.

SECOND AND THIRD TIER CONNECTIONS

Another myth that most people have about networking is that they don't know anyone who does a certain job, so it's not worth networking with them. Let's pretend that you're really interested in the field of mechanical engineering but you don't know any mechanical engineers. That's okay because networking isn't just about your first tier connections; it's about second and third tier connections. So, ask around and check on LinkedIn to see if anyone you know might know someone who's a mechanical engineer or works at an engineering firm you're interested in. It's highly likely that someone in your first tier of connections—your friends, family, colleagues, etc.—*will* know someone in that field or at that company. The tactic is to move to your second and third tier connections—whether you're using your phone, email, or LinkedIn contacts—and reach out and connect with these people.

Be specific about your ask

Here's another myth about networking: that other people might not want to talk to you about their jobs or themselves. In fact, many people are very willing to have a conversation with you to help you out if they can. Yes, people are busy, but if you are specific with your request, people are more willing and able to respond to your needs.

When you give people the specifics about how they can help you, you'll find much more success. You might say, for example, "I'm looking for a mechanical engineering job with a product development company in the Southeast. Do you know anyone that might be available to talk to me about their company or their role?" People will be much more likely to respond when you tell them exactly what you're looking for. But if you vaguely state that you're "interested in engineering," they won't quite know what to do with you, since there are numerous types of engineering roles. The more you can define what it is that you're looking for, the better.

Every day is networking day

When seeking a new career opportunity, create your own luck by shifting your mindset. Recognize that there is value in the conversations that you have with people you meet throughout the day. Rather than approaching each day in the same old way, start engaging more with the people you encounter. You *can* create positive outcomes, even just through these interactions.

When in job search mode, recognize that everything you do has networking potential. Striking up conversations and making connections is really all that networking is about. For example, the barista at your Starbucks and the receptionist at your dentist's office are valid contacts; you never know who (or when) an opportunity will present itself. When it's time for you to start putting your message out there, allow it to happen every single day.

Networking is everywhere! ◑

It's also helpful to remember that networking can happen in any situation. All it takes is engaging anyone you meet in friendly conversation and using it as an opportunity to pitch your areas of interest. For instance, when you're asked, "How are you?" or "What have you been doing?" answer with honesty and positivity, and say more than just "I'm doing great." Let them know what you're doing in your job search. Speak in the present tense and answer with something like, "I'm excited to be pursuing a role as an event planner!" Whatever your target role or target area is, speak openly about it in all of your conversations.

Here's another example. You're at the dentist's office for your routine cleaning and the hygienist asks you what you'll be doing over the next few months. Rather than saying "Oh, not much. Same old stuff!" consider responding with "Well, I'm excited about pursuing a career change and I'm working toward a new role as a (fill in the blank). If you know of anyone I might talk to in this field, I'd appreciate learning more." Your dental hygienist might just have a friend who has a friend in the career role or field you're pursuing, and she can initiate an informational interview between the two of you. Success!

Guess what? You just engaged in networking! It's all around you. You simply have to shift your mindset about it and engage in honest conversations.

It's not about you

It might seem counterintuitive, but *networking is not about you.* Yes, you do want to let people know that you're in job search mode during the course of your conversation, and what you're searching for specifically. But allow the discussion to take its natural course and talk in general about common interests or anything else that comes up. Better yet, keep directing the conversation back to the other person. The goal is to listen and reflect upon the input. People generally remember a conversation as being wonderful when they do most of the talking!

Networking doesn't have to be formal

As you're discovering, networking doesn't always have to involve a formal event, such as a conference, where hundreds of people have gathered to discuss trends and perspectives of a specific field, following by shaking hands and formal introductions. You can also network when you're volunteering, at a community event, while you're chatting with other parents at your child's soccer game, in an art class, or while you're in an educational seminar or workshop. *If you are in a room with two or more people, then you can network!*

To start networking today, ask yourself: *What am I going to do today?* Am I going to be at a community event or a training workshop? Am I going to be at the doctor's office or a luncheon with members of my sorority? All of these are opportunities to put your goals out there and to let others know of your targeted job search, because you never know who that person is or who they know. And if you don't engage them, then you could miss a promising opportunity for yourself.

I particularly like to suggest that job seekers look at volunteering and continuing education activities for networking because they allow you to grow as an individual while you're having conversations with like-minded individuals. If you're filling boxes for a local food drive, you might be standing next to a new, strong contact. So keep putting the word out there and being authentic about it. The right opportunities will very likely find you.

Start small. Gain confidence. Then branch out!

If the thought of large, formal networking is a little off-putting to you, then start by going to something small—especially if you're an introvert! Local business groups frequently have round table meetings, in which eight to ten people get together for breakfast or lunch to share ideas and connections. Find ways to have small conversations and build on that success. Ask people to join your network on LinkedIn afterwards. Then you can go to the next level, like stopping into a networking event where there are 50 or a 100 people. Challenge yourself but also be realistic with a stepping stone approach.

Of course, you can also network through professional associations, workshops, and seminars, all of which are things that you should be participating in when you're in growth or search mode. You can join groups on LinkedIn and start participating in them by sharing articles of interest. Once again, authenticity is the key; remember to engage others about themselves, rather than only broadcasting your needs.

Exercise 12: Contact your contacts

Make a list of 50, 75, or 100 contacts from your phone and email lists. Then, star or highlight those people who are connectors or rainmakers in your world. Since you already have your elevator speech and target role (right?) then, depending upon your level of comfort, craft an email or phone call script for contacting these key people. Ask them if they know of anyone at X company or in X field, and if they would be willing to get you in touch with the other person for an informational interview. Again, you're not asking for a job—although that opportunity presents itself occasionally! You're simply beginning to put out feelers and let others know about your search. If you do decide to email, make sure to craft individual emails to each person on your list. Nothing invites apathy more than a mass email.

Another strategy is to pick out one or two periods of time in your upcoming day when you plan to be open about your career goals. Plan out how you'll respond when someone asks you how you're doing. Once you feel comfortable and are able to do this with some ease, then move on to the harder things, like attending seminars, community gatherings and more formal networking events.

PRINT RESOURCES

Although it seems old-school, there are some print resources that can be very useful in the job search. Don't waste your time with the Sunday paper; but there are some other print resources that may be helpful. Depending upon your sector or area of interest, newsletters, professional journals, or professional publications may be fruitful. For instance, many professional organizations regularly distribute a professional newsletter or journal that may contain job ads.

Another helpful publication is the local business paper, such as the Atlanta Business Chronicle. A publication from the local chamber of commerce or a business chronicle can give you all kinds of information, like which companies are moving to the market, who bought what, who's expanding, and so forth. When you see an article about a company of interest that is expanding, for example, you could go to their website and look at their job listings.

Exercise 13: Looking at print ❶

If you choose print resources as one of your tracks, then obtain copies of your local business chronicle (a *Book of Lists* is even better if one is published for your area) and circle those companies and roles that are of interest to you and are aligned with your targeted job search. Gather up as many journals and publications as you can from the professional associations in your areas of interest, and then do the same.

Not the same old tired online job boards

Specialty job boards are the place to be for targeted job searches. Most of us have been brain-washed to believe that we need to look up the traditional online job boards. Truth is, they no longer meet the needs of the savvy job seeker. Since you're looking for a specialty area of expertise, you're probably going to have to look beyond the same old offerings. For instance, an employer at an innovative, growing company may choose to only use the company website to post jobs, and that means you wouldn't find that job on that-tired-old-job-board.com. But specialty job boards might contain some of those kinds of listings and so they are valuable for a targeted job search.

Start by looking into the professional associations that are linked with your area of expertise; membership may provide you with access to career resources. And many of these professional associations also endorse a specialty job board. Find the organizations that are aligned with your particular profession or area of specialty and see which job boards they might endorse. New job boards like Muse.com are fantastic for the start-up and technology sector, for instance. Flexjobs.com is another useful one for virtual and freelance jobs. There is a vast array of specialty job boards out there; you just need to search for yours.

Exercise 14: Specialty job boards ◑

If you've chosen specialty job boards as one of your tracks in your job search, then make a list of up to five job boards that might apply to your areas of expertise.

Metasearch sites

Metasearch sites are different from those tired old job boards, too. Like Indeed.com and LinkedIn.com (who partners with SimplyHired.com), metasearch sites use your key words and location of choice as guides to aggregate results from many areas, including company websites. Linkup. com claims that it ties into company career pages and gets direct access to company career portals—and that's a great thing for targeted job seekers like you.

Exercise 15: Metasearch sites

With your specific areas and keywords in hand, explore a few opportunities in your geographic area on metasearch sites and be sure to experiment with advanced search features.

COMPANY RESEARCH

Beyond networking, the top proven approach to finding a job is by researching companies you're interested in working for. You'll start by exploring the companies themselves instead of the specific roles or titles that the company might show as available on their web site. Why? Because if you can find an environment and setting that has potential to be a really good fit for you, then it's possible to network your way into that specific company and pursue the role that's best for you. For some it may be hard to imagine, but once you've defined what you want, then any time you make contact with a decision maker at a company of interest you can initiate a connection and potential job lead. Or perhaps you can even demonstrate your unique value and find that a role can be created for you, or a planned new position can be moved up on the timeline.

With this approach, it's more likely that you'll find job satisfaction and want to remain at that company. To help you with that, when you're researching companies, be sure to link up your values exercise with your research. Go after the settings and environments (as opposed to the role) that match your interests, and that way you may very likely find a better fit.

Start by looking into directories of companies for your area like the *Book of Lists*, which is a listing of organizations, by sector and category that is published every year for major metropolitan markets. Start extracting names and URL's of companies in which you're interested. Also check out chamber of commerce directories for your geographical area or city. If you need more help, try going to the library and asking a librarian to help you find specific directories. Librarians love questions! You can also do a Google search for "company directory for _____" or "industry directory for _____" and see what's out there.

Exercise 16: Company research

Draw up a list of ten companies that you'd like to investigate further. Once you've exhausted those ten, draw up ten more.

RECRUITERS

Recruiters can be another swath of color on your painting that shouldn't be overlooked. On the other hand, don't rely solely on recruiters as your only track to your best-fit job. There are two key types of recruiters. The first consists of *contingency recruiters*, who are paid by a company to find suitable candidates for their available positions. The second type consists of *retained search recruiters*, who are paid by job-seekers to represent them and place them within their industry or sector. They generally cost several thousand dollars. I recommend working with contingency recruiters because most people aren't in a position to spend that kind of money for a retained search firm.

NOT A TARGETED APPROACH

Using a recruiter is not usually part of a proactive and empowered job search. Keep in mind that with both recruiters and job boards, you can only be presented with the jobs that those entities have available. The odds are even lower with a recruiter than a job board, because the recruiter is only looking to fill a specific set of jobs.

Many people make the mistake of thinking that a recruiter will be able to guide and help them in the job search. But recruiters are not coaches or career counselors; a recruiter's role isn't to try to get you a better fitting position for yourself. A recruiter's job is to fill the available position and get paid for it, so they look at what you represent on paper and match that with key criteria in order to serve you up to the client. If you're a civil engineer and you want to go into sustainability, for example, then a recruiter won't necessarily be interested in finding a new role for you; they want to sell you based on what you've already been doing, based upon what they read in your resume.

That isn't to say that a recruiter can't or won't help you; but you shouldn't rely on them completely, especially if you're in transition or moving to a new field. Put another way, hiring a recruiter for your targeted job search is like going to the breakfast buffet and asking for blueberry crepes. When the manager says, "We don't have crepes, but I can give you a waffle and you can put some blueberry jam on it," if you really want the blueberry crepes, you'll leave the buffet and find a restaurant that offers mouth-watering crepes.

More Professional Help

Depending upon the circumstances surrounding your career transition, you might have started to think about hiring someone to help you. If so, you can choose among a variety of professionals, such as counselors, career coaches, career consultants, or resume writers (or a combination of the above).

A professional counselor will focus on the diagnosis, treatment, and healing of psychological disorders, often stemming from the client's past. The goal of counseling is to provide treatment to support the process of healing and growth. A counselor or therapist is the best choice for those who are dealing with unresolved feelings, emotions, and psychological issues that act as barriers to positive development. Issues might include anxiety, burnout, attention deficit disorder, depression, conflict management, and low self-esteem. Counselors have an advanced degree and are licensed by the state in which they practice. Many also maintain national certification.

A career coach or consultant often guides their clients through a process to assess their background, challenge boundaries, explore options, define goals and develop a plan of action. Using a developmental model, career coaching poses the following core questions, "Where are you now and where would you like to be?"

Like counselors, many career coaches are skilled at administering and interpreting formal career and personality assessments to gather data in key areas such as skills, strengths, interests, values, and preferences. A career coach may also be highly skilled at developing targeted resumes and letters. An effective coach maintains certification from a national professional organization. Many have also completed a graduate degree program.

Finally, a professional resume writer helps people to prepare their personal marketing materials, with a clear focus on targeted roles in a specific industry. They will critique your current documents and work with you to prepare materials that highlight your strengths, expertise, and professional achievements. Many resume writers also have national certification.

When selecting a professional for yourself, consider their experience, credentials, affiliations, and client recommendations. A complimentary phone consultation is standard practice; be sure you have a clear understanding of the terms of the services to be provided.

Beyond price and professional background, be sure to get answers and insight to several key questions:

- What is their specific training and experience in career development?
- What professional credentials do they hold?
- Will you feel comfortable interacting with this individual?
- Do they offer virtual sessions/services, in person or both?
- Will they represent your best interests?
- Will they act with empathy?

EXERCISE 17: CHOOSING A PROFESSIONAL ◑

First decide what type of professional you'd like to work with (if any): a recruiter, coach, counselor, resume writer, or a combination of them, and then begin to research possibilities. Remember that you are the most valuable commodity, so ensure that they are working towards your goals and have knowledge about your areas of interest.

INFORMATIONAL INTERVIEWING

While I covered informational interviewing extensively in Chapter 1, I bring them up again to emphasize that they're a great way to get the inside scoop on a particular career role or a particular company. I usually recommend trying to talk to two or three people in roles in which you're interested in order to get better scope and perspective. Just to reiterate, though, remember to be genuine when you approach people about informational interviews. If you try to disguise an intention to get a job within a request for an informational interview; you'll come off as disingenuous and the whole thing will likely backfire. Instead, treat the informational interview for what it is: real world information to fuel your job search. ◑

PROFESSIONAL ASSOCIATIONS

Professional associations often have career resources on their websites, as well as publications or newsletters, as I've mentioned previously. In addition, they often offer seminars, workshops, webinars, and conferences that you can attend. One of the first things that you might want to do in your job search is to become a member of associations that represent your desired area. Then you can attend their seminars and workshops and look into the professional designations and requirements for certifications. Some professional organizations may even have mentoring programs, which can be a boon for you as an emerging or transitioning job seeker.

Exercise 18: Associating with associations ◑

If professional associations are one of your chosen tracks, then seek out resources—both in print and online—that they offer. Begin to narrow your focus to the resources that you want to pursue. In addition, see if there are any upcoming networking meetings, seminars, or workshops that you'd like to attend. Make sure to record everything on your log sheet.

ALUMNI ASSOCIATIONS

We often forget about our alumni associations. We might even think of them as a kind of nuisance. But there have been changes for the better in what alumni associations offer to their members, including more ongoing assistance and professional development, career development, and networking opportunities. Some even provide resume critiques and career development webinars that might be valuable to you.

At the least, most alumni associations have alumni databases, which can allow you to link up with other alumni and do some networking. Tapping into this network to set up some informational interviews is a great way to make a connection; people are usually very proud of their alma mater and very willing to help other alumnus.

Exercise 19: Accessing your alumni association

Take a look at the services your alumni association offers. Does anything stand out? Is there an alumni group on LinkedIn that you can join? Does it have mentoring programs or networking groups? Publications or resources? Make a list of the items that are of interest to you and add them to your log sheet for further review.

TEMPORARY, PART-TIME, CONTRACT, AND FREELANCE OPPORTUNITIES ◑

Going the part-time or freelance route is a great way to test-drive your chosen career. It can make it easy for you to move slowly into another profession and even pick up some extra money via your freelance work. You get to take a career for a drive and see what it's like. Further, the experience might grow and turn into an offer for a full-time opportunity or even turn into your own venture.

Exercise 20: Consider freelance

Imagine what part-time or freelance work might look like for your chosen area of expertise. Does it strike you as doable to add in some of this work to your current schedule? Are there times in your week that you may be able to fit in a couple of extra hours?

CHOOSING YOUR TRACKS

The number of job search tracks that I've listed in this chapter may be overwhelming to you at first, but like the martial artist and her work to achieve a more polished throw, we can break each track down into discrete, doable chunks. Moreover, no one would expect you to engage all tracks, but ask yourself if there are three, four, or five that make sense for you. The more tracks you activate in your job search, the more resources and connections you gather, and the more ground you ultimately cover in your search. ◑

A WEEKLY STRATEGY FOR FOCUS AND SUCCESS

When they decide to get serious about their job search, some optimistic job seekers proclaim, "I'm going to work 20 hours per week on my job search!" But most people don't really have 20 unclaimed hours a week, especially if they're already working another job. The best method for keeping focus and persistence in the job search is to schedule your time in realistic blocks or "chunks." This will help you maintain focus and avoid any sense of being overwhelmed.

The strategy I recommend here helps you create a weekly routine you can follow that will streamline your search. You'll set aside blocks of time on Mondays and Tuesdays to accomplish one set of activities, time on Wednesdays and Thursdays for another set of activities, and you'll set aside a final block on Friday. As each chunk of time is devoted to a certain mode or activity, and none other, you'll find that the consistency and focus will make your tasks easier to manage, help keep you sane, and get you results more effectively.

- **Create a log sheet**

Start by creating a log sheet. I recommend you use Excel if you can, but you can also do it with pen and paper. Create columns at the top of the page for each of the following:

Company Person Title What When How Notes

- **Monday and Tuesday: Research mode**

Find some blocks of time for Mondays and Tuesdays, about 45 to 60 minutes, and put it in your schedule as time you'll use for searching and researching. But—and this is important—only do research during that time, like circling interesting companies in a business chronicle, or reviewing the specialized job boards for your areas of interest. Or research people with whom you'd like to have informational interviews. Any of these ideas will do, but be sure to limit yourself to one at a time; don't hop back and forth between many. This approach helps you keep your sanity, helps you stay focused, and gives you feedback that you're moving forward. As you identify things to do, keep a list by writing them down, printing them out, or bookmarking them on the computer.

To keep track of your to-do list, create an action folder, either virtually, or the old-fashioned manila ones! You will need it for the next stage of your focused work.

A great use of your Monday/Tuesday time might be to research print resources, specialty job boards, metasearch sites, company research, as described in Exercises 13 through 16 above.

- **Wednesday and Thursday: Production mode**

On Wednesdays and Thursdays, you'll go into Production Mode where you'll use the information from your research on Monday and Tuesday, and take action. Set aside about 45-60 minutes on both days. Then, whether it's setting up an informational interview with someone, or writing cover letters and completing multiple job applications, it's time to knock them out. Since your research was very focused on Monday and Tuesday, your production experience can be focused and constructive. Go through your folder of action items and take the necessary steps to advance and complete each item until the folder is empty.

- **Friday: Follow-up activities**

Same thing. Designate a block of time to follow-up with the resumes, job applications, informational interviews, and networking activities that you accomplished last week (5-7 days earlier). Can you now make a phone call for the jobs that you applied for? Or can you send a follow-up email? Whatever step you take, document the activities you complete and any feedback you receive on your log sheet. Whichever method you're using— manual log or digital spreadsheet—document everything, like jobs you've applied for, people you've spoken with, and contacts you've emailed.

This strategy creates a focused flow through the week for you and helps you avoid the scattershot approach to the job search. For example, if you were in research mode and you spotted a job that you liked and then immediately stopped to apply for it, then you would have derailed your search and research time. Or, if you're rushing to get an application out, then you might make unnecessary mistakes in the process, and you would've lost the time that you had set aside to do research on other companies and roles.

People often get into this scattershot mode when they think that they have to apply for a job as soon as they find one. But you don't; the job isn't going to disappear in a matter of a few days. Companies are usually seeking the best candidate for a position, not the one who happened to spot the job first. So it's better to stay in your search/research mode and then move to production later in the week. This way, you can get five (or more) applications out the door in a week, which will keep advancing your search strategy and keep you from being overwhelmed and frustrated in the process. As long as you are doing what you need to be doing, and staying focused on your targeted role, the right position will materialize.

FOLLOWING UP

Follow-up is usually the toughest part of a focused job search strategy and deserves its own mention because it usually comes with a fear of rejection. Yet like everything in the job search, follow-up is all about your mindset. If you can keep focused on moving through your log sheet and following up, instead of wondering what you'll do if they say No, or entertaining other negative patterns or beliefs, then you'll be way ahead of the game.

It may help to keep in mind that whatever response you get during a follow-up call or email—you don't need to take it personally. Easier said than done, right? But ask yourself what's worse: being rejected by someone you love or being rejected by a stranger? If the person on the other end of the phone or email chain is curt or snippy or abrupt with you—no big deal. If you get cut off by an HR manager? No problem. You're doing your job and they're doing theirs.

Today's system of recruiting talented employees isn't designed for you to get through to a decision-maker, so follow-up takes tenacity and persistence. Start by pulling up the HR page of a company with whom you're trying to follow up and see if you can speak to an in-house recruiter or in-house HR rep. Then make the phone call. You might make it all the way to a human being, or it may be a voicemail. If you can't get through by phone, then send an email. Of course, if you're told in the job posting, "No phone calls" then you have to respect that and not make any phone calls. If you do get through to a person and they say that they'll get back to you, then write that down in your log sheet and move on. Again, don't take it personally.

Here is wording I recommend for following up: "Hi. I'm calling to check on the status of my application. Is there any additional information that I can furnish to support your review of it?" Or, "Can you tell me where I am in your process and what I might expect as a time frame for next steps?" Always be polite, always be professional, and always know that you are just as worthy a candidate as anyone else out there.

You can also try to find the name of the hiring manager or decision maker, and once you've submitted the standard application, you can send an email or snail mail with your resume and cover letter to that person. If you go that route, mention in the cover letter that you've already applied through the applicant management system and that you wanted the opportunity to also reach out to him or her personally.

Exercise 21: Setting up and using your log sheet

As described above, create your log sheet, either on paper or using Excel (a downloadable version is available on the website).❶ Then, create your schedule for the next week. Find a 45 to 60 minute block of time on Monday/Tuesday, Wednesday/Thursday, Friday, and maybe a little time on the weekend. Pick an area that you'd like to begin your research for your Monday/Tuesday session, and then follow along with the rest of the program.

Getting Unstuck from a Job Search Rut

Many years ago, when I had risen to the rank of *sankyu*, the first level of brown belt awarded in judo, I decided to step away from judo classes and training for a few years as I began to focus my attention on college and starting a career. But in my early 30s, I was inspired to resume my judo training by a gifted physician, George, a national judo champion from Egypt. George rekindled my love of judo and I soon found myself joining a small club to take weekly classes. The members of the dojo gave me a very warm welcome and my body had to quickly reacquaint itself with the strength and flexibility it would need to practice judo. I attended classes on Wednesday evenings and Saturday mornings and often visited my parents on the weekends. I'd arrive at their home with a slight limp in my step and I often winced in pain when I sat down or rose from a chair.

As is common with many martial artists, I routinely applied icepacks to the bruises that adorned my toes, ankles, shins, wrists, elbows, and shoulders. It was not uncommon for parts of my body to glow with the color of a ripe eggplant. On one Saturday afternoon, following a judo class, I was at my parent's home, applying yet another icepack to my bruised shin. My mom walked in the room, stared at my swollen, purple shin and asked, "Is all of this really worth it?"

Without hesitation, I responded, "Yes! Because I'm learning. And judo brings me joy."

My mom gave me a smile and said, "Then I'll get you another icepack," and turned to leave the room.

As you go about your job search, you might start to feel that you've hit a rut and you can't get any further. It's natural to have highs and lows in the job search process. When you hit a slump, try your best not to berate yourself or get caught up in "what ifs," "could haves," and "should haves." It's critical to generate some creative energy, motivation, and inspiration to propel you out of any lows that come along.

To do this, start by taking a short break from your search. Find simple ways to change your weekly routine. Get out of the house, engage with people in your network, and introduce yourself to fresh surroundings, people, and activities. You never know where inspiration might strike. Need help jump-starting some creativity? A simple but often powerful exercise is to reflect upon the books, websites, and magazines that most often pique your interest.

Now take this exercise a few steps further. Adjust the speed of life a bit by slowing things down if you're feeling stressed or stepping up the pace if you need to get your heart beating a little faster. Consider spending a few hours at the library, a museum, a historical site, the theater, or one of countless other environments to stimulate your brain. Maybe you need a jolt of endorphins that comes from a bike ride, a jog, an extra workout at the gym, or a simple walk in the park with your pooch on a sunny day. Go to a coffee shop to write in your journal, take a co-worker to lunch, or invite a friend to join you for dinner as you prepare a new recipe.

Internet job boards and company career sites will wait if you decide to step away from the computer for a few more hours each week. Once you've allowed yourself to step outside of your routine, you may find that a dose of objectivity can inspire bouts of creative brainstorming.

CHAPTER 4: BROWN BELT

INTERVIEWING

"Learn from yesterday, live for today, hope for tomorrow.
The important thing is not to stop questioning."
—Albert Einstein

Interviewing often looms large in the minds of those searching for work. Yet an interview can be a powerful way to discover more about your best career fit. In judo, we learn that by routinely testing the skills we've been learning, we master the ability to deflect and defend against the moves of our opponent. Likewise, the interview is a great place to test out whether an organization is a good match for you. You can glean information about a particular company or organization; you learn about the interviewer just as the interviewer is trying to learn about you. In a judo match, you'd scan your opponent's energy; in an interview, you scan an organization and see where you would fit within their culture.

To give yourself a more comfortable mindset about interviewing, think of the interview as an opportunity to talk with the company and learn more about them. In your mind, you can even replace the word "interview" with the word "chat," as in "Company X has invited me in to have a chat with them." That feels better, doesn't it?

Three factors in the interview have a lot of influence on your success. The first factor is the likeability factor: how much connection your interviewer feels with you. The second is psychological, or what you're thinking as the interview plays out, which also influences your mood and energy. The third, of course, is content: the answers you give to the questions you're asked.

THE LIKEABILITY FACTOR

The likeability factor comprises at least 50% of the interview and has to do with intangibles like whether or not you come across with confidence and professionalism. Your interviewer is much more likely to move you to the top of the list if she finds you genuinely likeable. That includes whether she believes you have the right personality and can see you in the organization as part of their department and part of their team.

If this worries you, fear not. The good news is that with the right type of preparation and a new mindset, you can become more confident with your answers, convey a professional demeanor in your responses, and exude likeability. Rather than worry about whether or not someone likes your personality, focus on how much the positive aspects of your personality shine through.

THE PSYCHOLOGICAL FACTOR

The psychological component has to do with how confident you are. When it comes to interviews, many people fear the unknown. They worry that they don't know what the interviewer is going to ask and they don't know if they'll have a strong answer. But while you can't predict exactly what your interviewer is going to ask you, you can use the methods described below to give you much more confidence to answer any question, and help you let go of the fear. While you have absolutely no control over what you'll be asked in an interview, you do have control over the quality of your responses. When you're authentic in the delivery of credible information, and feel somewhat assured about your responses, then you'll be confident about how you come across to others. Keep in mind that confidence Is expressed along a spectrum, falling somewhere between insecurity and arrogance. The goal is to strike a balance in which your interview preparation allows you to build confidence without inflating your ego. Many people have a lot of fears, worries, and anxieties, and their minds fill with questions like these during the interview:

- The interviewer has all of the control in the process.
- If I crash and burn on this interview, then I'll never get another interview.
- This is the only job I'll find.
- Will I meet their expectations? Will they like me?
- What if I do something embarrassing, like sweat profusely or babble?
- What are they going to ask me?
- How will I know what the format is?
- What if they ask me something I can't answer?
- What if I'm not properly prepared?

Notice that each one of these ideas is only a thought in your mind. As you become aware of these anxious thoughts, you can start to counterbalance them and create a new mindset.

Stopping negative thoughts

One of the best and simplest methods I've found for refuting anxious thoughts like these is called *thought-stopping*. Dr. Albert Ellis, who developed Rational Emotive Behavioral Therapy (REBT), encourages us to use thought-stopping as a means of replacing anxiety-laden, often irrational thoughts, with more rational, calming thoughts. It works for many situations, not just interviews.

Start by becoming aware of your thoughts about the interview; writing them down is even better. Then, counter each thought with a different thought, one that feels more comfortable and emotionally beneficial. For instance, if you're thinking, "I might get so nervous at the interview that I start sweating profusely, or completely forget what I wanted to say, or stumble over my words." Then develop a rational thought that contradicts these thoughts. You could review how many times you've actually been in a situation where you were sweating profusely; or you got so nervous you got sick to your stomach; or so nervous that you completely forget what you were trying to say and couldn't actually recover. For many, it's never actually happened, right? Or maybe it happened once in the fourth grade? Either way, the odds of it actually happening to you while you're in an interview are slim. So now you can use the rational thoughts: "The odds of that happening are pretty low, and I've never actually had that happen," in order to replace the negative, anxiety-laden thoughts.

Now that you've seen how to replace a thought with something more rational, then you can start to use the negative thought-stopping technique whenever an anxious thought pops up. If you're thinking about the interview and you hear your mental chatter saying to you, "Oh, no, I'll completely forget what I'm going to say," then that's your chance to tell yourself: "STOP. That's not a rational thought, that's not going to happen."

Byron Katie, a well-respected writer and speaker, offers a similar approach using four questions that can further help you to see these irrational thoughts for what they are: irrational. You can tune in and say to yourself:

- Is that true?
- Do I absolutely know that it's true?
- What if I no longer believed that thought?
- What would my life be like if I let go of this thought?
- Once you've answered those questions, then you can then replace the thought with a more rational thought like, "If I do my homework and prepare properly, then I'll have a strong base from which to speak."

You will be relying upon your preparation from each of these three components above as you approach the interview.

Before your interview

Now that we've tackled the anxiety-producing thoughts you might have during an interview, let's also go through a process that you can use just before the interview. Take a few moments beforehand to visualize success. Go into the bathroom if you need to, or take a few moments in your car, and visualize the most amazing interview ever. First go to your "happy place." Mine has always been walking on the beach. Close your eyes and take a couple of deep breaths and start relaxing into that place. Hear the waves and the sea gulls, smell the salty air, feel the mist on your face. Use all of your senses to go there. Then picture yourself in an interview that is going really well, one in which you're prepared for an array of questions and you answer smoothly and with confidence.

And *then* go into the interview.

By the way, play the part from the beginning. *Turn it on and turn it up.* Be nice to everyone, as soon as you drive onto the campus, including the guard at the gate, the main receptionist, the administrative assistant—everyone. Treat the janitor the same way as you would treat the CEO.

Beginning the interview

As the interviewee, your job is to make the interviewer feel comfortable. (Yeah, sorry!) So as the interview starts, quickly assess and match the style of the interviewer. If you can, reflect on the thinking and feeling scale from Myers Briggs (MBTI). For instance, you'll know pretty quickly if your interviewer is a thinker, because he or she will try to get you to convey data, numbers, and will ask you to quantify things. They'll ask logical questions, they'll want quantifiable information, and they won't express a lot of emotion. You won't get questions about rapport, motivation, teamwork, and so on. So if you're a feeler and you're talking to an engineer, then speak from the quantifiable sides of your experience.

On the other hand, if you start hearing questions about rapport, conflict negotiation, atmosphere, or culture, then you're probably dealing with a feeling-oriented interviewer, and you'll need to speak more to the "people" aspects of your work. Focus on teamwork and collaboration, how you build rapport, consensus, giving people a voice, and similar topics.

If you're reading your interviewer's style accurately, and responding to it, then you'll notice your rapport with the interviewer build and improve. And the interviewer is likely to find you more appealing (more likeable!) at the end of the interview than if you had just stayed with your natural preference. The smart interviewee will adjust accordingly and match the energy in the room.

Some people ask me if this approach is being fake. My answer is that, no, you're setting yourself up for success by delivering your message in a way that will be most comfortable to the interviewer.

During the interview

When the interview begins, you'll want to sit comfortably in your chair and open up your posture so that your diaphragm isn't crushed. Also, if you tend to jiggle your leg or tap your foot, try sitting up straight in your chair, and imagining that your feet are anchored or glued into the floor and that you can't move them. You can also press the balls of your feet into the floor. The interviewer won't be able to tell that you're doing that, and the visualization will help to calm the tapping or jiggling. And if you tend to use your hands, try holding onto a pen, like you're ready to write at any time. It will anchor your hands.

A common nervous habit is to create a verbal pause with "um", "ah," and "like." It's the equivalent of your brain trying to keep going. But try something different. Instead of using these verbal pauses, or anything else you might use to fill in a pause, take the tip of your tongue and press it to the roof of your mouth. It will make it much less likely that you'll want to keep talking. This simple technique prompts your brain to just pause and not fill in the space. (By the way, if you think that you don't ever say "um" or "ah," you may just not be aware of it. Be sure to ask your practice interviewer about it.)

Ending the interview

If you're really interested in the job, then say as much at the end of the interview—and perhaps throughout it! You can say something like: "Based on everything that you've told me, I believe I'd enjoy contributing to this organization. I like everything that you've told me about X, Y, and Z, and from my research, I'd really like to work here. Is there any additional information I can provide to support my candidacy?"

Be sure to get business cards from the people conducting the interviews, if possible, or at least from the most senior person or lead on the panel, if it's a panel interview. If someone doesn't have their card available, then ask if you can obtain their contact information from the administrative assistant or receptionist so that you have a way to follow up.

After the interview

As soon as possible after the interview, send a Thank You card via traditional snail mail. Most people will just send an email, so this is another chance to make a great impression. A card makes a much stronger impact than an email and helps to make you memorable. Also, a real *Thank You* card shows that you're interested and that you're professional. The card can also give you the opportunity to clarify or reinforce a response, such as, "I don't think I fully answered that question or particular topic, I want to add X." Whatever you write, keep it very short.

People like receiving real mail, and a *Thank You* card enhances the impact that you made on the interviewer. Think of how interesting it is to receive an odd-shaped or colored envelope in your mail (especially at work!) You'll want them to remember the good stuff from the interview, and a *Thank You* card often builds positive energy.

Is there ever a reason to send an email instead? Sometimes you might want to give the employer something extra and juicy, for instance a plan describing what you would do with your first 30 days on the job, or something you might have read that applies to what you discussed in the interview. Or, you might want to add something to what you've said. In these cases, you can definitely email them with that information. However, an email and a *Thank You* card don't have to be mutually exclusive, and your correspondence should always start with the hand-written *Thank You* card.

Don't forget to take some time for reflection. Right after the interview, while it's still fresh in your mind, revisit the interview. Write down what you think you aced and where you might have fallen short. See where you can improve your performance or improve your stories. You want to use every interview as preparation for your next interview. In this way, your performance gets stronger each time.

What about follow-up? Schedule a time to follow up with the company a week to 10 days after your interview. A phone call is best. On the call, you could say, "I wanted to check on the next steps in the process. Is there any additional information that I can provide to support my candidacy? When might you be making a decision on the next steps?" If you can't reach the people with whom you spoke, then go ahead and leave a short voicemail. If you can't get through on the phone or even on voicemail, then send an email with the same follow-up questions.

Follow-up can be another area of anxiety, but you can simply decide not to buy into the anxiety about the possibility of being rejected. After all, the system isn't designed to welcome job seekers as candidates; it's designed to keep them at bay. So if you put the energy out but you don't get a response, don't take it personally. Just make a notation in your job search log and then move on.

One more thing. If you see something in your interviewer's office, like a diploma, trophies and awards, pictures, a piece of art and the like, then use it as a means to connect. You've got a whole environment around you that you can draw from, so use what's there in order to make a clear connection with the person on the other side of the desk.

Behavioral-based interviewing ◑

Behavioral-based interviewing is one key to presenting the confidence you seek. At its core, it is about telling stories about your experiences, to fulfill your interviewer's assumption that the best predictor of future performance is past performance. You'll want to convey to your interviewer how you have thought, acted, and produced in the past so that they can weigh those facts against the demands of the position.

For example, in a standard interview, you might get a questions like, "What is your greatest strength?" It's a tired old question, for sure. The behavioral-based equivalent question would be more like, "Tell me about a time when you had the opportunity to engage one of your top strengths."

But, what if your interview starts like that? The answer is that even if the employer is asking you standard questions, you still answer with a behavioral response. You tell a story. For instance, you could say, "Let me give you an example of a situation in which I was able to leverage one of my top strengths." No matter what the question, you respond with prepared stories and paint a picture for the interviewer about the effectiveness and success in your background.

If you get the prompt "Tell me a little bit about yourself," you'll want to give your elevator speech as a response. If you already have one prepared, and you've practiced it, then you can adapt it to the person before you.

THE CONTENT: TELLING YOUR STORY

Let's face it, there's nothing fun about interviewing—for either party. It's a challenge to be met by the candidate and a necessary task for the interviewer. But if you can tell goods stories, it will be a refreshing change for them and you'll be more memorable in their minds. And that's always a good thing!

So how do you tell great stories about your past experiences? Just like you would sit down with a friend and chat over a cup of coffee, you give details and background of all of the sights, sounds, and experiences of the stories you tell. You have to make it believable for the interviewer. You help them experience your story as if they were there.

Here's a formula that I recommend that helps you tell great stories. I call it "Situation –Assessment/Actions – Results," or S-A-R. You may have seen something similar presented elsewhere as the STAR technique; S-A-R is a variation that I formulated to help my students and coaching clients. With this formula in your back pocket, no matter what your interviewer asks you, you'll have a defined method to answer her question.

Here's how to use it. First, find a couple of job postings for the jobs you're interested in and print them out. Then, take a highlighter or a red pen and circle the key words or phrases that point to things the employer is looking for in a strong candidate, such as skills, strengths, technical skills, competencies, personal characteristics and traits.

Now create a worksheet. (You can also download a S-A-R worksheet from the website.) You'll have three columns, titled Phrases/Keywords, Examples, and Draft, respectively. Start by listing each item you've identified in the job posting(s) in Column 1. In Column 2, jot down a note about any time you remember when you've displayed that specific skill, strength, or quality.

Then walk away from the worksheet for a day or two. When you come back to it, pick the one example or situation out of the ones you've jotted down that best represents that area, expertise, quality, or trait, and circle the one that you've chosen.

Now, using the examples/situations you've selected from the previous step, flesh out your stories by giving one or two sentences to each of the three parts: Situation, Assessment and Actions, and Results. Finally, for each skill you've listed, write down the situation under "S," your assessment and the actions you decided to take under "A," and the results you achieved under "R." While you're writing, pretend that there is a camera in the room and create a robust story with many details and descriptors. Don't just say, "Well, I had this project, and it was the first time that I had the ability to use analytics, and I presented it to the client, and they were happy with the results." Tell the listener who your client was, what sector were they from, what they liked specifically, how big the project was, if it global, if you interacted with other teams, what your thinking process was, what analytics program you used, how you presented it, and so on. Those details are what will make your story interesting to the interviewer and make you memorable. If you give them predictable answers and tired old language and phrases, then they won't remember you and you won't make as much of an impact as you could.

Once you've got the meat of your ideas down, it's time to put your stories on 5x7 index cards. While your draft may have been on paper or in Microsoft Word, you still need to transfer everything over to 5x7 cards. Why? The smaller space forces you to encapsulate the story and lock down the key elements. It forces you to be concise; you don't want to take three minutes to answer questions in your interview. That's the kiss of death. Each story should be no longer than 60 to 90 seconds; the 5x7 cards ensure this conciseness.

Use one card for each skill, and write the skill at the top of the card. For instance, if one of your skills is conflict management, then write "Conflict Management" at the top of the card. Then write the letters S, A, and R down the left side of the card, one under the other, leaving some space in between them for the information you pull from your draft page.

Index cards are also great because you can review them anywhere and you don't need your computer to do so. Writing them down also ties into basic learning theory: if you write it down, and then practice with the resulting flash cards, then you have a much greater ability to retain the information. *Flash cards work.*

Try starting with four flash cards, and then go to six and then eight. You'll eventually go into the interview with 15 to 20 stories to tell. (It is much easier than it sounds.) The goal isn't to memorize the card and spit out the contents in a rote manner; the goal is to retain the core of the story and to deliver it just as if you were sitting down with a friend, having a glass of wine, and telling a story. That takes practice. So you may want to practice with a friend, spouse, or coach.

Negative-sounding stories are okay

Don't shy away from negative scenarios for some of your stories. In fact, a couple of your stories *should* describe negative situations. You might mention the one in which you were asked to work on a team that you didn't like, or a situation in which your strategy didn't work, or a client who wasn't happy with early results, and so on. Don't be afraid to tell those stories if you can demonstrate how you learned, how you quickly adapted, and how you turned things around. You always want to be selling your results.

Sculpting these stories can conquer those fears of not knowing what the interviewer is going to ask or whether you'll be able to answer them. Even if you don't know what they're going to ask, you can still make some strong educated guesses based on the job posting. And even when you're not prepared for a specific topic area, then the stories you have written down are still with you, allowing you to immediately move to your own experience, use the S-A-R skeleton/frame, and then tell the story.

Of course, it's also helpful to prepare an S-A-R response for many of the standard interview questions, such as:

- Tell me about a time you had a conflict with a co-worker.
- Tell me about a time you disagreed with a directive from your boss.
- Describe a situation in which you believe you were producing your best work.
- Give me an example of when you believe you exercised a key strength.
- How do you develop rapport and collaborate with co-workers, peers, supervisors, clients, etc.?

All of these examples actually come down to one question: Will your personality, work style, and strengths mesh with those of the team members and culture of the organization you're applying to? If you believe the role could be a good fit, and you're prepared to do your homework, then you'll benefit from having numerous stories available to express the value and fit you offer the organization.

Being a convincing story-teller

Part of acing the interview process comes with recognizing that the interview involves some acting on your part. You have to emote. You have to make good eye contact, you have to smile, you have to come across as relaxed and confident, and you need to be able to make small talk. So if you're telling a story that's kind of funny, then you have to smile and laugh a little bit. If you're talking about conflict management, then you need to be serious and crinkle your eyebrows. If you're feeling energized, then you need to show it on your face.

The credible and interesting stories you convey help to make you a memorable candidate. By emoting and giving your potential employer the personality and the energy that matches your stories, you offer information that is believable and draws the interviewer in to you. At the end of the day, you want to be memorable. You don't want the employer to look at the manila folder that contains your resume a week later and not be able to remember anything about you.

Having confidence isn't egotistical

Some of us may feel funny expressing ourselves and emoting, especially when we're talking about ourselves. Introverts in particular have a hard time talking about themselves; they sometimes feel like they are bragging or being arrogant. If you have that worry, it's helpful to realize that you're only providing an employer with credible details about what you've accomplished. You are engaging in self-promotion; you're *not* being boastful or allowing your ego to fill the room with statements like "I'm the best Excel user that you've ever seen." Confidence is just telling a good quality story, and once you've prepared yours, it will become much easier. Of course, if you're an extrovert, you'll likely bring natural energy and enthusiasm to the interview. Just remember to provide credible details to your stories.

One technique to help you get accustomed to telling your story is to grab your favorite book and read aloud for 20 or 30 minutes. This is a proven technique for introverts, or for anyone else, for that matter, who wants to strengthen their verbal communication skills. You can do it either sitting or standing up: simply read with emotion. Use your voice and facial expressions to give emotion to the characters and key details. Really tell the story, remembering to breathe and to pause. Also think about the speed at which you're reading so that you're speaking at a reasonable pace. You may want to either record yourself or have a friend or family member listen to and assess your pace, volume, pronunciation, tone, and emotion. You can even try reading to your kids if you don't already; kids love emotional story-telling and play-acting. Obviously, you will adjust the emotion and tone when speaking to adults in an interview.

What to do when you don't have an answer

Many job-seekers fear they'll be asked something that they don't know the answer to once they get into an interview. Maybe they haven't worked on a certain type of project, haven't been in certain situations, or haven't worked with a particular technology yet. Many simply fill the gap by talking about an experience that comes close to the topic of the question. That's one approach. Another approach is to fib, which you should never do.

My recommendation for when you're in this situation is to tell your interviewer how you *would* get the answer or *would* approach the situation. Give them an example of your thought process in order to obtain a resolution. For example, if you're asked about your experience with a specific software platform that you have not used yet, you could come back with an answer like: "I would reach out to my network to get some feedback on the platform. I would perform internet searches to find solutions and I would look into some focused learning, perhaps on the vendor's website, for a webinar or one-day seminar."

By telling the interviewer your approach, you tell them how you would think, act, and function in less-than-perfect situations. You're providing the interviewer with a behavioral answer, and that is what they are most interested in anyway.

Exercise 22: The S-A-R process ◑

Start your S-A-R process. Begin by finding examples of job postings and circling the key skills you believe match your background. Then flesh out your stories.

Questions for the interviewer ◑

Here's another question that many dread in an interview: "Do you have any questions for me?" But if you've done your values list, peeled back layers of information from the organization's website, and have gathered feedback from your network and from online reviews, then you'll have questions for your interviewer, based on your values list. You'll want to better understand the environment and the culture, and you'll want to find out if the organization's values align with yours. If these questions haven't already been answered, you can ask about the core responsibilities of the job, the mission of the organization, the work/life balance, and so on. Did you decide that you would only travel 10%? Then you'll want to ask questions about how much travel is involved. By looking at your values list, you can come up with questions that will allow you to get feedback on how your values (must haves and desired elements) will align with the organization's. Also consider these key questions:

- Can I meet one-on-one with a member of the potential work team?
- If I come on board, how will the organization set me up for success?

You'll likely have a list of 10-15 questions to ask your interviewer about the organization, but be sure to prioritize them. You're only going to be given a few minutes to ask your questions and to find the right opportunities to interject them. You may want to spread your questions out across the interview process, potentially in two or three meetings.

The salary discussion

Many job candidates are terrified to answer the question, "What are your salary requirements?" If you are a strong candidate for the job opening, then your work commands a fair salary. But what is the definition of "fair"? The initial interviews are usually not the place for salary negotiation. I'll talk about that more in a later section.

However, you should be prepared for salary questions just like all other types of questions. Do your homework and research websites and databases, preferably those offering search parameters for your industry, and gather salary ranges both for the positions that you've held and the ones that you're pursuing. Consider your level of education, experience, the size of the organizations you have worked in, as well as your geographical location. You need realistic, "real-world" data to negotiate effectively. Also, use Google searches and information from your network, professional associations, Payscale.com, Salary.com, and Glassdoor.com to come up with the numbers. Then, when the question comes up during the interview, you can provide a range instead of a specific number. Your range should start slightly above your "rock bottom" number and end up a bit above your expectations. It will give you wiggle room for negotiations going forward in the process.

These days, you might get asked questions about salary requirements electronically before you even set foot in an interview, in a cover letter/ email response, or within the organization's online applicant management system (AMS). Using the range you have decided for yourself, you can decide what number to select from that range, based upon the situation. If you are submitting the application via email, you might present a salary range in your cover letter or email body. If the application is being submitted online (via AMS), and the response box is a required field, you must select a number you're comfortable defending. Whenever possible, qualify your response by stating that salary is certainly negotiable based upon the total compensation/employment package. And if the response box is not a required field in the AMS, I suggest skipping it all together, putting you in a better position to negotiate in the future.

YOU'VE BEEN OFFERED THE JOB! NOW WHAT?

It is very flattering to be a chosen candidate for a job opening. However, don't let the excitement cloud your judgment about the important question of whether or not the position is a better role or a better organization for you. You'll still want to consider: Are they offering a solid employment package based upon your background and potential value that you offer? Is it an organization and role that truly aligns with the information you've gathered from the four cornerstones (skills/strengths, values, personality and interests)?

If you've done your homework by researching and clarifying the role that will fit best for you, and you feel like you've interviewed the company as much as they interviewed you, then you should have a good sense of whether the role is something that you want to accept. But it's also good to check in with yourself with meditation (if you practice it) or simply by sitting in silence for a bit and asking your body how it feels about the role. If you are carrying tension, if your gut is knotting up, or if you can't seem to shake a sense of unease about the company, then take a step back and realize that there are other options, and that being given the opportunity doesn't mean that you have to take it. If this feels a bit too fuzzy or New Age for you, then making a Pros vs. Cons list with the information you've gathered on the role and the organization will allow you to reflect further on the offer.

If you do decide it is the job you want, then if your research tells you that the salary or benefits don't quite match your expectations, then you still might have room for negotiation. Keep in mind that when people accept a position at a salary level they think is low for someone with their experience, they often end up feeling undervalued, and job dissatisfaction builds quickly. So make sure you are asking for all that you deserve by negotiating from a friendly position of strength. You've obviously developed a good rapport with your interviewers if they've offered you a position, and you can use that to your advantage in a kind and respectful way. Continue your dialogue in a professional and courteous manner and learn as much as you can about the perspective behind their offer. You can use this information to respond with quantifiable data to support your request. Discuss or revisit your credentials, background and career accomplishments and re-emphasize the contributions you believe you can make to the organization, both short-term and long-term.

But don't focus on salary alone; consider the complete employment package you're being offered. Elements of the package may include:

- paid time off (PTO) as vacation, sick, and personal time
- paid holidays

- an annual stipend (or reimbursement) for professional society memberships, professional development, or continuing education
- paid portions of employee insurance (individual or family coverages), such as health, dental, vision, and disability (short and long term)
- retirement or 401k/403b
- employee evaluation checkpoints and potential corresponding pay increases
- profit sharing
- bonus/incentive plans
- tuition reimbursement allowance
- wellness programs
- flexible working arrangements
- a company vehicle or mileage reimbursement
- use of company equipment and facilities
- discounts with vendors/organizations who have partnered with this employer

If, during the course of your negotiations, the employer will not budge on the initial salary offer, consider bargaining with them to add a few more items to the total benefits package. Since the employer does not have to pay matching payroll taxes on non-salary benefits, see if they might consider an additional three to five days of paid leave each year, or an annual allowance for association memberships or professional development activity, such as seminars and workshops. Maybe they would be willing to add a sign-on bonus after the initial three to six months of employment or a performance bonus at 12 months. They might say "No," but it won't hurt to ask.

One of my clients was told three times during the interviewing process that there was no room in the budget to increase the starting salary. When he received the job offer, we were able to negotiate an additional $3K of salary and perks.

Also: be prepared to walk away. If you do not receive an offer that is at least equal to your minimum requirement—a salary level that will allow you to meet your monthly budget—then be prepared to walk away. A new career role offers the opportunity to rekindle your enthusiasm and creative energy for work. But when the pay is too low, your motivation will drain pretty quickly. Plus you'll be more stressed due to your struggle to pay monthly bills.

Once you accept a job offer, you will need to discuss the start date, the onboarding process (new employee orientation and enrollment in employee plans and programs), training and work schedules, travel requirements during the orientation period (typically 90 days), plus supervisor feedback and evaluations during the initial months of employment.

Focus on establishing good communication practices with the organization's representatives right from the beginning. It will allow you to gather feedback about their expectations and compare it to your perspective. You can discuss gaps in the information you received during your onboarding, within the orientation period, and throughout the remainder of the first year of employment.

YOU WEREN'T HIRED! NOW WHAT?

Finding out that you weren't chosen as a final candidate for a position you've interviewed for can be deflating and a blow to the ego. But the same resiliency lessons that we talked about in pre-interview mode are just as important (if not more so) in this scenario. It's helpful to root out any thoughts in your head that aren't serving you, like, "Well, of course they didn't pick me. I'll never have the right skills and experience," and replace them with something else. Here are some helpful replacement thoughts. Pick one, memorize it, and then every time one of the defeating thoughts pops into your mind, repeat the refuting thought to yourself.

- *A better fitting job is out there for me.*
- *If this wasn't the right role or organization, it's better that I know now.*
- *I am qualified for many jobs and wouldn't have gotten this far in the process if I weren't qualified.*
- *I have the ability to improve my knowledge and skills every day.*
- *I see myself in a job that looks like _____.*
- *In what ways can I be more creative, more tenacious, and more resourceful as I continue my search?*

THE JUDO OF LEARNING

Martial artists soon learn the old adage, "Fall down seven times, get up eight." In Career Judo, you use the interview process to reflect on anything that you might want to improve on in the future. Of course, you need to be careful not to use the experience as an opportunity to beat yourself up. For instance, if you notice that you get nervous beforehand, you can remind yourself to learn the calming techniques for your next interview. Each stage of your process can provide another helpful message and point you in the direction of where you ultimately want to be. By taking the time to calmly analyze an interview, you can see the areas that you might need to improve, or the qualification or skills that you need to beef up on, before you are fully aligned with a role that fits you well.

It's also a good idea to approach your feelings about not getting the job with a little bit of humor. Give yourself a reward for all of your hard work. Use the thought-refuting techniques when fears crop up and then move on to the next one! Your better-fitting role is out there!

In the words of Jigoro Kano, the founder and master of judo, "Judo teaches us to look for the best possible course of action whatever the individual circumstances."

CHAPTER 5: BLACK BELT

ADVANCEMENT

"Action is the spark that ignites potential."
– J.E. Long

After years of training, the day finally came for my black belt exam. I was in judo class, and my sensei stopped the usual practices and called me to the front of the dojo. He announced that I would be testing for my black belt and all members were welcome to observe the process. Artur, my training partner (*Uke* in Japanese) and I knelt in front of the class as I responded to an array of questions from my sensei. It was the oral portion of the exam: I was to convey my understanding of judo's history, terminology, and protocols. When that was complete, the sensei barked out commands for me to demonstrate a series of techniques and forms.

After about an hour, I once again knelt in front of the class, this time quite exhausted. Sensei announced to the class that it was his honor to award me the rank of *shodan*—the first degree (*dan*) of black belt in judo—as he handed me a new black belt. I removed my tattered brown belt and tied my new black obi around my waist. Many years of training and practice had led to this moment and I was overcome with pride and exhilaration.

Most people think of advancement as moving up the career ladder in a rigid hierarchy, by getting promotions, on a regular basis, and that's certainly one way to advance. But advancement might also involve working with or leading a team that you're interested in, or doing your own thing as an entrepreneur, or freelancing on the side. If you're truly ready for "advancement" in your current job, try to open up to all possibilities.

It's helpful to define what success means to you specifically. The media's definition of success is usually about having more money and collecting bigger and more expensive things. But what about the highly admired preschool teacher who loves her work and might never make more than $25,000 a year? I still say that she is a success.

Ask yourself what success means to you. Is it about landing a high-ranking job title and making $300k per year? Are you a success when you're driving a luxury car to your vacation home in the mountains? Or do you want to feel engaged and empowered in your job, be admired by the leadership, be the best salesperson in the region, have your students enjoy and recommend your classes, or be respected by your peers? I challenge my students and clients to take time to reflect upon what is truly meaningful and important to them in life. The allure of money, possessions, prestige, and influence will likely always exist. Yet in your desire to consistently enjoy a sense of accomplishment and appreciation in your work, I believe it is equally important to reject stereotypical definitions and define your personal picture of success.

What is your goal? Positive psychologists, such as Martin Seligman, Ph.D., recommend that we focus on what is right, what is good, and what is working in our lives as goals for growth and living a more authentic life. Seligman's PERMA model describes Positive emotions, Engagement, Relationships, Meaning, and Accomplishments as key determinants of well-being and happiness. The model points to

PERMA

Positive Emotion ▢ Engagement ▢ Relationships ▢ Meaning ▢ Accomplishments

intrinsic goals: the ambitions that motivate you from the inside and aren't based on external rewards such as money, title, and material things. For example, most people want to make more money and list that as a primary goal. But what, exactly, would more money mean to you? Does it mean that you'd have the ability to travel, to have more free time with family, and to pursue your hobbies or freelance projects? Is that performance bonus somehow linked to your vision of added respect from your coworkers? I have had numerous clients who believe they are a success in their career, yet they were experiencing a lot of frustration, complacency, and burnout due to the intensity of their weekly work schedule. They might admit that their salary level is tied to their self-esteem, but it's more likely their ego. These clients often flounder when I ask them, "What would you pay to recapture several hours each week to have more personal time to enjoy a hobby, a recreational sport, to spend time with a loved one, or to simply relax?" For these clients, if you divide their salary by the number of hours they are actually engaged in work activities each week, the math reveals the shrinking value of their time from working 60, 70, even 80 hours a week. Again, I urge you to use your values as a source of motivation to craft your personal definition of success.

Exercise 23: Your best life

One simple way to get in touch with your vision of success is to journal about your best life for 20-30 minutes. Picture yourself one to five years in the future and describe what you're doing, who you're surrounded by, and how you're acting as you go about your day. Imagine the sights, sounds, and experiences playing out for your future self. Be in a place where anything is possible, where money is no object, and where you have exactly what you need to succeed. Consider it like a fairy godmother exercise: I can give you your dream job: just tell me what it is. Write down as much detail as possible without editing or reviewing. And then look back over what you've written and see how it matches with the path that you're currently traveling. You may want to circle back to your earlier values exercise and see if anything new arises.

PURSUING LEADERSHIP ROLES

When people hear the word "leadership," it often freaks them out, especially if they're just starting off in a new industry or heading into the workforce after college. But leadership doesn't always have to imply that you're aiming to be CEO. Being a leader can also mean serving on a committee, directing a project team, volunteering to take charge of a program at a non-profit organization, or simply taking on more responsibility in your current work, to gain more diversity and breadth of experience. It's all up to you.

There are countless non-profit and volunteer organizations actively looking for help and talent. Advocacy groups in particular are very open to working with people from the community who are willing to take on leadership responsibilities. Of course, if your goal really is to move up the ladder at work, then think about what you need to have or do in order to advance. What types of skills or qualifications do the people in leadership roles have? Where do they spend their time? This will look very similar to the exercises that you've already done for determining gaps.

Promotions don't necessarily appear out of the clear blue sky. If you want to lead a team, consider leading without being asked. Show leadership during meetings by listening to all viewpoints and promoting inclusion and collaboration. Lead small informal mentoring groups. Participate in company-supported affinity groups, like those for minorities, women, LBGT, and so forth. Take the lead on committees and teams, even if they aren't directly work-related. And be sure to work through the processes listed in Chapter 6. By taking responsibility for your actions, including your thoughts and reactions to others, then you show that you are ready to lead.

TEACHING AND MENTORING

Many black belts in judo reach a point where they decide to start refereeing, coaching, or teaching. After learning a lot from their judo masters, they want to give back to others. You might be thinking along the same lines, no matter how far along you are on your path. Consider the newest interpretation of Abraham Maslow's "Hierarchy of Needs," a well-respected representation of the needs that motivate human behavior. What if we were to move beyond self-actualization, which Maslow suggests is our highest need: our ability to evolve into the person we wish to become? Perhaps we can rise even higher, ultimately to transcendence, helping others to self-actualize—often through teaching, leading, mentoring, and giving back.

Where can you help others evolve, and what will nurture your own sense of meaning and purpose in life and career, by doing so?

Wherever you are in your career—that's exactly where you can start to give back and help others on their journey to self-fulfillment. You don't have to be a black belt or a member of the C-suite before you start teaching, mentoring or being of service to others. The question is, what can you offer *right now*? What do you know how to do really well? What system, process, software, soft skill, people skill, crafting, sports—or whatever—do you know and want to teach to others?

You could teach others how to set up a LinkedIn profile, how to use

Powerpoint or Excel, how to learn a sport or how to write a book. You could teach accounting principles, how to organize a closet, or how to design a warm and welcoming room. Whatever you love to do or are interested in, other people will want to hear about it! Even if you are just launching a career or post-degree venture, you have skills and interests that others may want to learn.

Don't wait to be asked. Seek out places to give. Try community groups, youth groups at your place of worship, primary schools, continuing education, or elder hostels like the Olli Center for senior learning. Investigate opportunities like senior retreats or underserved groups. No matter what your skill set, there's someone out there who would enjoy your energy, presence, and service.

By teaching others, we learn about ourselves. Volunteering and advocacy don't need to be relegated to the category of "things that I'll do sometime in my life." They don't lack in relevance just because you're not paid for doing them. In fact, positive psychologists have proven that volunteering and helping others in any way nurtures us and provides more meaning in our lives.[1] That increased meaning contributes to a sense of positivity and well-being. To put it another way, we're happier when we help others!

Exercise 24: Where can you give? ◑

Examine what it is that you enjoy doing or do well. Do a Google search for a few areas in your community that might welcome volunteers. Then send them an email to let them know of your skill set and availability. You might also check out a targeted web site such as Volunteer Match (https://www.volunteermatch.org/) or other sites offering to help connect volunteers with organizations.

---

[1] Baumeister, R.F., Vohs, K.D., Aaker, J.L. and Garbinsky, E.N. (2013). Some key differences between a happy life and a meaningful life. Journal of Positive Psychology, 8 (6), 505-516. http://dx.doi.org/10.1080/17439760.2013.830764

BECOMING AN ENTREPRENEUR

If you're interested in striking out on your own, but the thought of being an entrepreneur seems too scary, then think about "hanging out your own shingle" in a different way. Could doing your own thing mean working part-time on the side in an interesting sector until you develop your product or service? Does the idea of freelancing or being an independent contractor with an already established business appeal to you? How about becoming an advisor, consultant, direct marketing representative, coach, or trainer? All of these roles are entrepreneurial yet you're not necessarily working all alone; you'll likely have interaction with clients and team members.

Just like leadership, it's helpful to step away from the stereotypes about what an entrepreneur is or does. If you know that being an entrepreneur is in your future, but you don't quite feel that you're there yet, what would it take to push yourself toward that goal? You can begin by researching resources in your area for entrepreneurship and small business development and by looking for networking opportunities with other entrepreneurs or with people in the industry you're interested in.

If you decide to pursue your own venture and your own path, then you don't have to feel alone: there are many resources out there for you. You don't have to fear that you don't know how to do this or that part of running a business; there are numerous small business resources, incubators, and workshops to support you. (And thank goodness there's always Google and YouTube.) You're not expected to be an expert in all of these areas; use the resources that are out there to your advantage. If you have the idea, energy, and determination, keep identifying credible resources to set yourself up for success. ◑

Pick something that speaks to you and just start. There are no wrong choices; you can always refine or change what you're doing later on if you find that you don't like your original idea or if it's not working out. You can't help but learn something in the process, even if it's not immediately apparent.

And just like the job search, if this all seems daunting, then take baby steps. Seek out volunteer opportunities, try an internship, go to workshops and conferences, and talk to people in the field you're interested in.

Exercise 25: Questions for an entrepreneur

If you feel that you're ready right now, but you aren't sure what you want to offer exactly, try these questions for brainstorming:

- What process, system, or product does the world most need right now?
- Have you gained expertise in a hobby, sport or craft that may point to a business venture?
- If you had to put your idea on a billboard or banner, what would it say?
- What do your friends tell you that you are really good at?
- How can you best serve others?
- What type of challenge would you like to take on?
- What is something that you can offer right now, today?
- Have you already created some process, system, or thing that you use successfully that might be of benefit to others?
- Where or with what do you get frustrated and what could you do to transform that frustration into an idea?

CHAPTER 6:
BEYOND THE BLACK BELT
THE MINDFUL CAREER

"Change is the end result of all true learning."
— Leo Buscaglia

A shining highlight of my years in judo took place on the day I attended a training clinic for brown belts and black belts near Brockport, N.Y. The guest instructor was Dr. Sachio Ashida, one of the most respected and highest-ranking judoka in the United States. Dr. Ashida immigrated to the United States from Japan in 1953, completed a Ph.D. from the University of Nebraska, and became Associate Professor of Psychology at the State University of New York, Brockport, where he also led the university's judo club. To me, Dr. Ashida represented the essence of judo. Meeting him was like being in the presence of royalty. He was small in stature yet his presence filled a room as he instantly garnered attention and respect with a gentle, commanding demeanor. His comments and instructions conveyed words of wisdom that I cherished. I ended the day with a deeply-felt respectful bow to Dr. Ashida. I was all together exhausted yet enlightened and felt that I had grown both as a judoka and as a person.

As you go forward with your own career, you might realize at some point that career growth—and finding meaning and fulfillment in your role in life—requires ongoing discipline. We don't just stop once we've landed in a new job; we want to learn more, grow more, and expand into all that we do. A black belt doesn't stop learning once she's gotten the belt. Quite the contrary: she deepens her knowledge by continuing to practice, stepping forward, and exploring new areas for growth. All of which is to say that one of the best things that you can do in your new role is to adopt a growth mindset. Tell yourself that you're going to learn all that you can, and then some, about your role and your place in it. Humans are engaged when they are learning, and the latest research says that we can learn at any age. Turns out that we're all capable of neuroplasticity: developing new neural pathways to support our brains.

As we grow, we also want to determine how to nurture ourselves within our current role. For help with that process, we can look to positive psychology for the tools it offers. More than merely about teaching us to be "happy," positive psychology helps us to work towards building a life that focuses on meaning and engagement as well as feelings of pleasure (Seligman & Steen, 2005).

Numerous studies have shown that the tools of positive psychology— like appreciation, gratitude and grit—increase our chances of success and our overall job satisfaction. Studies have also shown improvements in attention and creative thinking skills when mood and happiness are at a higher level (Rowe, Hirsch, & Anderson, 2006). Said another way, we're able to be more creative, build greater resilience, and get more stuff done when we use the tools from the world of positive psychology. ❶

FINDING FLOW

In judo, we seek to achieve a state of flow, the point where we're moving without effort or forced thought. In the career world, flow can also be a state to which we can aspire. The concept of flow was first coined by Mihály Csíkszentmihályi. Essentially, it describes a state of mind in which what you're doing is effortless, and you're mindful, you're engaged, and you're excited about the activity.

When we desire greater career satisfaction, we want to seek out roles that allow us to experience flow as much as possible. It's not likely that you'll be able to escape all the mundane elements of your work entirely. But if you can cultivate and nurture opportunities for more natural engagement and flow, your work can become more meaningful. It will help you become more aware of a career path that fits you best.

Exercise 26: Getting in the flow

Write down three recent examples of when you've felt entirely engaged at work, when time had passed quickly, and you felt a sense of accomplishment and meaning.

POSITIVE THINKING SKILLS

Even if we push forwards and do everything that we're supposed to, sometimes we still feel like we're treading water and the world is against us. But the secret to living a career (and a life) filled with purpose and meaning is that we have to make changes in our internal dialogue.

Let's take a fictional example. Michael recently gave a presentation to a room full of people. Afterwards, his boss met with him and ran through a couple of key points that he could have improved on, as well as the highlights of the report. Michael was upset that his boss didn't seem to take him seriously or respect him, and stormed back to his office. But then he took the time to sit down and remember that his boss was generally very pleased with the presentation and his work overall, and that she only wanted to help him to improve. She didn't think that he was unfocused or unprepared after all; he had only read that into what she said. So Michael apologized for his reaction and worked on the report again, incorporating her input.

That's resiliency. Resiliency can be helpful in many situations:

- Before giving a presentation
- To improve your mood after a bad day
- Before speaking with a difficult colleague
- After having a tough call with a client
- To deal with a fear of failure
- Applying to a job, even when you've heard nothing back from the previous 19
- Signing up for a certification program
- Going on yet another job interview
- Being tapped to lead a project or for a promotion when you don't think you're ready
- To deal with fear of success
- To neutralize self-sabotage

All of these situations are kind of important in the career world, right? To become more resilient takes being able to refute self-defeating thoughts and fears that spring up, to persevere even when you have low energy, and to know that your path may not necessarily look "safe" or "normal" to others around you. Resiliency is defined as "the ability to bounce back from negative events by using positive emotions to cope." At its heart, it is about refuting and overcoming patterns of negative thinking.

How to become resilient

Remember those self-defeating thoughts I listed in Chapter 4? Thoughts like "I can't do this," "I'm not strong enough," and "I'm not smart enough"? The way to resiliency is by countering those thoughts. You look into the actual thought that is going through your mind as to why you can't do something, and then you write down a statement to clearly disprove it: a reason that your thought might not actually be true.

For example, if you think, "I'm not smart enough to run an entire department," you can look at all of the times in your life that you've had a similar thought or feeling. (I'm not smart enough to get into college, or to pass that honors course, or to make the President's list, or to pass that certification exam, etc.) Remember how you did persevere and achieve, despite your fears.

When we're forced to think about it, we usually already have some examples of our resilient nature; it just needs to be recalled, claimed, and explored. After you've disproved a negative thought, you can even peer into it more deeply and understand what you learned from the challenge: What was the learning and the growth there and how are you now stronger for the experience?

Challenge your thinking with "what" questions

Another way people get sucked down a negative rabbit hole is when they continually ask themselves why something is happening. It's a sure-fire way to bring yourself down and to allow your thinking patterns to make you ineffective.

Here are some that might be familiar:

- "Why is this happening to me?"
- "Why is this happening now?"

- "Why isn't my plan working?"
- "Why can't I reach my goal?"
- "Why am I feeling this way?"

We ask "Why" questions because we want to understand or reconcile a situation. But is the question being driven by a need to learn and grow or is it an emotional response? Often a "Why" question is referred to as the "victim's question." It's as if we're asking, "Why me?" "Why" questions tend to focus on what might or could have been instead of what could be improved by going forward with a more proactive approach.

What instead of Why

Consider asking "What" rather than "Why" questions. Laura Berman Fortgang, a leader within the field of coaching, brought a lot of light to the value of asking "What" questions. She refers to them as 'WAQs'— Wisdom Access Questions— on the side of the head. WAQs take you beyond information gathering to concentrate on outcomes and solutions. When you have a goal in mind, you can do the research to help you make informed decisions that can propel you forward. After all, the future is where positive change and goals reside. Here are some examples of essential and compelling "What" questions:

- "What needs to change?"
- "What resources can I explore?"
- "What's blocking my path?"
- "What negative patterns am I repeating?" For example: job hopping
- "What do I need to demonstrate to be seen as a leader?"
- "What do I need to learn or accomplish?"

Think of a common scenario, such as a conflict with your boss. You might ask questions like, "Why doesn't my boss like me?" "Why does my boss treat me this way?" Or even, "Why is my boss such an ass?" I'll admit that these questions are good for bitching and whining. But the fundamental problem with these questions is that they have much more to do with the other person and their behavior than they have to do with you. You can't spin your wheels trying to figure out the other person's thoughts and motives. Instead, try asking yourself something like, "What can I do this week to improve my relationship with my boss?" A "What" question allows you to be proactive and to seek out a solution.

Grit

You might recognize the term from a favorite book, movie, or news story. Grit is perseverance and passion in the service of long-term goals, even in the face of obstacles. Having grit doesn't mean that every stage of your development looks like fun. Think of a single mother, getting up every day to write another thousand words for her novel, or a bookkeeper going to night classes to complete a Bachelor's degree in accounting, when she'd rather be out with her friends, so that she can make the next promotion at work. That's grit.

According to researchers, grit entails working strenuously toward challenges, maintaining effort and interest over years despite failure, adversity, and plateaus in progress. A gritty individual approaches achievement as a marathon; his advantage is stamina. Whereas disappointment or boredom signals to others that it is time to change your trajectory and cut your losses, the gritty individual stays the course and remains focused on the goal.

The research[2] on grit shows that grit is the main determining factor for success, more so than intellectual ability, family background, or perceived talent. This is awesome news: it means that you don't have to be the smartest or most talented in your field, only that you have the determination to discipline yourself to keep working toward what you want.[3] With grit, you continue to do your work in a focused manner, look for ways to improve, keep a watch on the leaders and trends in your field, and continue to push forward toward your goal.

GRATITUDE

Numerous studies[4] confirm the power of gratitude to boost happiness in a big way. It can occur "in the moment thankfulness"[5] or in the form of regular, even daily, gratitude exercises. Any way that you practice it, gratitude means taking the time to recognize and be aware of the good things that are already going on in your life. We tend to focus on our packed schedules, our stress, the perceived lack of time, finding that we have overcommitted, and being stretched too thin. But taking a little bit of time to appreciate what you already have can make a tremendous difference in your morale and outlook.

Gratitude can also help you to recognize the other side of the coin in situations that are daunting or overwhelming. For example, if you're starting to feel stressed by a new project you were given, you can think, "It's nice to be appreciated and respected by others. By giving me a new

[2,3] Duckworth, A., Peterson, C., Matthews, M.D., and Kelly, D.R. (2007). Grit: Perseverance and Passion for Long-Term Goals. Journal of Personality and Social Psychology, 92 (6), 1087–1101. http://dx.doi.org/10.1037/0022-3514.92.6.1087

[4,5] Tugade MM, Fredrickson BL, Barrett LF. Psychological Resilience and Positive Emotional Granularity: Examining the Benefits of Positive Emotions on Coping and Health. *Journal of personality*. 2004;72(6):1161-1190. doi:10.1111/j.1467-6494.2004.00294.x.

project, I am being recognized for my strengths." There's always something to appreciate, even in the toughest of situations. It just might take us a bit of time and reflection to find it!

Exercise 27: Ideas and reflections log

Rather than keeping a traditional journal, you might like the simplicity of an Ideas and Reflections Log. First, pick out a blank notebook with a cover design that speaks to you. Then, every day, write down either three good things that happened that day, or three things that you're thankful for in your life. Try to keep it going for 30 days. For extra credit, try writing down some of your negative thoughts—such as, "I never have enough time for myself"—and then write down the other side of the coin. For this example, you could write, "It's really great that others see my strengths and expertise and reach out to me for help."

ALLOWING

In judo, we take the momentum from our opponent and redirect the energy. We don't resist; we let the energy flow around us. In life, we're asked to do the same by being present, being in the moment, by practicing mindfulness, and by not worrying so much about how things will be accomplished. We call this *allowing*. It's when you give yourself permission to be in this space right now, just exploring, and allowing. No need to judge yourself or others or the situation. Simply allow new experiences to come to you without needing to analyze or categorize. Allowing means trusting the process and believing that there will be a positive outcome; you put out the energy and focused thought with a specific intention and then remain mindful of the opportunities that start to present themselves to you. You may have heard of another term with a similar meaning: *getting out of your own way.*

In the career world, allowing can sometimes by perceived as laziness or as something that we should resist. People should push forward on their desired path with full action, right? But what if we didn't? What if we could embrace other possibilities, perhaps even those we haven't acknowledged or seen yet, but are being offered to us by the universe?

Allowing goes hand in hand with intention-setting, but it's definitely the more difficult of the two. Many of us are capable of being clear about what we want, but we think that only through our own actions can we bring that thing or ideal state into being. We often forget that we are part of a huge interconnected whole and that other people will be there to support us.

What's the best way to practice allowing? It helps to set aside a dedicated practice time each day; make *allowing* the second half of your gratitude practice. Begin by reflecting and writing about things in your life that you are already grateful for, and then write about those things that you'd like to see manifested in your life. These might be physical things like a new car, or they may be intangibles, like being an expert in your chosen field, learning to play a musical instrument, or becoming proficient at a sport.

Does the practice of allowing mean that you should just sit back and allow everything to flood into your life? No. But it does mean that you don't have to push quite so hard. You don't have to allow action alone to determine where you go. You don't have to constantly strive for, push, and propel yourself towards something. Sometimes you can simply pivot and allow the energy to flow in a new direction…it may just yield some positive results.

It's somewhat paradoxical, but one thing to understand about allowing is this: as you put the energy out there to reach your goal, you let go of the need to control the outcome. If you were a skilled judoka, you would still regularly practice your throws and grappling techniques; and if you were an experienced writer, you'd still work on your writing skills. But once your work is done, you've executed the technique or you've completed the writing piece, you don't hold on to the results of your work. You release the work and the positive energy it holds, and allow that energy to unfold and experience what the universe returns to you.

Let me give you a more practical example. When I speak to potential new clients, I'm often asked how I measure the success of my career coaching. One common and disappointing fact of life in the kind of work that I do is that we coaches and counselors might never get to see the results of our work. Our clients move ahead with life, armed with new knowledge and resources, and often see no need to check back in with us to give an update. To me, it means that I must measure my success based upon the energy and intention I put into my work—and then I allow my client to do her part. Since I am not with her when she is applying for a new job, completing another round of interviews, sitting for a certification exam, or competing for a promotion, I must smile and focus on the fact that I know that she is better prepared after completing her coaching sessions compared to when she first reached out to me. I must allow my clients to muster their own energy, do the necessary work, follow the plan we've developed, and in turn manifest their desired outcomes.

Exercise 28: Telling it like it will be

When you take time to reflect and write, add in a few wishes for your life that you would like to see, writing them down as if they are already evident. For example, you could write, "I'm so thankful for being recognized with a promotion." Let yourself sink into the good feeling of having your accomplishments appreciated and feel excited about the possibilities afforded you in this new role. And if you feel yourself getting pulled into old patterns of negative thoughts such as, "Well, that will never happen to me," tell yourself to "STOP" and let go of that thought. Focus on the potential that awaits you and go back to the positive feeling of being recognized with a promotion. As I tell my clients over and over again, other people are enjoying a cool job, creating an amazing product, offering a unique service, or running an innovative business… *WHY NOT YOU?*

Where do I start?

"Changing my thinking? Starting an ideas book? Challenging myself with 'what' questions?" I know that all of these new ideas and suggestions might seem overwhelming to you at this point. Yet I hope you have learned from this book, that you can be proactive, embrace positive change, and quickly make progress toward your goals. You simply have to set the intention to start today and take the necessary steps as you reflect upon and refine the process of moving forward towards what you want in your life. Much like your career—which, no doubt, will unfold and evolve across your life-span—your journey of personal growth has no one, firm destination.

So start by getting yourself a notebook, and then pick one exercise that speaks to you and that you can complete each day. Try to start with just 20 to 30 minutes per day, preferably in the morning, and commit to at least two weeks without interruption.

As a professional coach and lover of the art of judo (*"the gentle way"*), I recognize that it takes work, focus, and intention to accomplish each goal. I congratulate you for that! I wish you growth and success as you explore all of the beautiful and abundant opportunities available to you.

"Be not afraid of going slowly. Be afraid of standing still." ~Eastern Proverb

ABOUT THE AUTHORS

JOHN LONG, ED.S., BCC, CMCS

CAREER & LIFE COACH

John is a professional coach, university instructor and *career transition survivor* (serving almost two decades in healthcare management roles). His private coaching practice has offices in Atlanta, GA and Jacksonville, FL. He specializes in career and life coaching, as well as the administration and interpretation of career and personality assessments. He also teaches undergraduate courses in psychology, human services and student success. John has completed an educational specialist (Ed.S.) degree with a major in counseling and educational psychology and a master of science (M.S.) degree with a concentration in career development. John's work with students and clients takes a strengths-based approach blended with elements of positive psychology and solution focused change.

John's professional credentials include:

BCC™ – **Board Certified Coach** (Certification #000016, Member of the Founding/Inaugural Circle): A national coaching credential earned through the Center for Credentialing and Education, Inc.; Greensboro, NC.

CMCS™ – **Certified Master of Career Services** (Certification #CA-3000322121): A competency based credential earned through the National Career Development Association - Credentialing Commission; Broken Arrow, OK. To be awarded the CMCS, an applicant must have demonstrated, via formal assessment, a mastery of the <u>CMCS Domains of Practice</u>.

CCSP™ – **Certified Career Services Provider** (Certification # CA-5814833529): A competency based credential earned through the National Career Development Association - Credentialing Commission; Broken Arrow, OK.

GCDF™ – **Global Career Development Facilitator** (Certification #GCDF05418-US): A national career coaching credential earned through the Center for Credentialing and Education, Inc.; Greensboro, NC.

CPCC – **Certified Professional Career Coach**: A professional designation offered to career coaches through the Professional Association of Resume Writers & Career Coaches; St. Petersburg, FL.

Certified MBTI® (Myers Briggs Type Indicator) Practitioner through the Center for Applications of Psychological Type, Inc.; Gainesville, FL.

Qualified Strong Interest Inventory® Practitioner through G/S Consultants; South Lake Tahoe, CA.

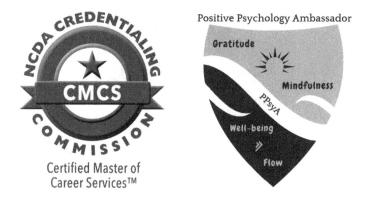

Certified Master of
Career Services™

Positive Psychology Ambassador

John's websites include: www.careerjudo.com, www.exploretworoads. com, www.exploretworoads.net, and www.positivepsychambassador.com

ERIN NEWMAN, LCC

MINDSET COACH

Erin is a *LifeWorks* Certified Coach who has studied the process of self-transformation and growth with many teachers. She helps women to claim their path and to find confidence and fulfillment in launching a business, much like she's learned to do in her own life's journey.

A graduate of the University of Virginia and a fluent German speaker, she spent many years in corporate America struggling to fit her round hole self into a square peg, and she's now found her calling as a mindset coach for aspiring entrepreneurs, working with individuals who want to turn their calling into a business.

Erin truly believes that each person already knows the answers within, and can find these answers by asking the right questions and listening deeply. In her coaching practice, she uses a combination of guided visualizations and insight to help each client discover how to step into authentic courage.

Erin has been certified as a Life Coach by the *LifeWorks School of Coaching*, as well as received one-on-one training with Dr. Jill Kahn of *Empowerhouse Leadership Consultancy*. Many spiritual practices, including Buddhism, Hinduism, and Shamanism, inform her practice and help others to heal. Her special gift of a <u>Confidence Booster Worksheet</u> is available at **www. Erinnewman.com**. And come join in the conversation for aspiring entrepreneurs in the *Dream Starters Community* on Facebook!

Printed in the United States
By Bookmasters